Pete Dulin

LAST

Bite

100 SIMPLE RECIPES

From
**KANSAS CITY'S BEST
CHEFS AND COOKS**

LAST BITE
100 SIMPLE RECIPES FROM KANSAS CITY'S BEST CHEFS AND COOKS

Edited by Pete Dulin

Photography by Roy Inman

Design by Eric Schotland

Published by *Kansas City Star Books*
1729 Grand Blvd.
Kansas City, Missouri 64108
All rights reserved.
Copyright ©2012 by The Kansas City Star

First edition, first printing
ISBN Print Edition: 978-1-61169-071-2
ISBN Ebook Edition: 978-1-61169-072-9

Printed in the United States.

To order copies, call StarInfo at 816-234-4636 and say "operator."

www.TheKansasCityStore.com

Suggested retail price: $17.95

 KANSAS CITY STAR BOOKS

CONTENTS

CONTENTS

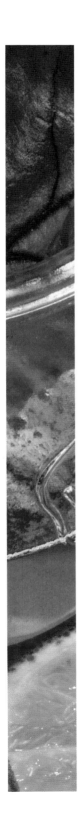

ACKNOWLEDGEMENTS

PETE DULIN

This cookbook would not be possible without the talent, hard work, and humor of photographer Roy Inman. It's a pleasure to work with him. Thank you to Eric Schotland, who designed *Last Bite*, and to publisher Doug Weaver at Kansas City Star Books.

My gratitude goes to *Kansas City Star* food editor Jill Silva and *Star* writer Cindy Hoedel, who contacted me over three years ago to coordinate and write the weekly *Last Bite* column in *Star Magazine*. Cindy served as the editor for *Last Bite* initially until Tim Engle took over the reins. Thanks to each of them for the opportunity and steady work.

Thank you and much love goes to Pam Taylor, Bennett, Alyson, and Delayna Muraski for the constant love, joy, support, and weirdness. Mom, Dad and the rest of my family, I love you.

Sheri Parr at The Brick and manager Adam Horner and Chef Tate Roberts of EBT Restaurant opened their establishments for the portrait sessions. Roy and I are grateful. Cheers to Bonjwing Lee for crafting the foreword.

My work at large would be nowhere without the support of editors, publications, readers, and friends past and present too numerous to mention.

Chef Philippe Lechevin gave me my first professional cooking job and introduced me to Le Fou Frog. Love always to Chef Mano Rafael, Barbara Rafael, and the Frog family for your support and soul-satisfying food and drink! Cheers to the chefs and cooks in this book and the many people in the service industry I've met over the years. You inspire me as much as the artists and musicians in this fine city. Here's to the next book where I can tell your stories.

Finally, the spirit and memory of Chef John McClure was a personal motivation for creating this cookbook to acknowledge and celebrate the abundance of culinary talent in Kansas City.

ROY INMAN

A big thank you to all the chefs who contributed their time, creativity, and expertise in the preparation of the recipes, and who many times accommodated the crazy, last-minute deadlines of a newspaper magazine. With Pete, I add my gratitude to *KC Star* staffer Cindy Hoedel and former features editor Mary Lou Nolan who gave me the opportunity to photograph the *Last Bite* feature in *Star Magazine* these past three years.

Pete Dulin is always a joy to work with. His keen comprehension of all things food gives him the ability to diagnose from a photograph what should or should not be in the frame. This skill saved me and *The Star* from embarrassment more than once due to a slip between the plate and the image sensor, so to speak. His careful attention to detail also negated the possibility of disgruntled readers.

And as always, much love to my dear wife Barbara who amazingly has put up with a photographer husband for lo these many decades.

FOREWORD

BY BONJWING LEE

I was born in Kansas City in the Seventies, raised there in the Eighties, left in the Nineties, and returned home in 2006, after ten years of schooling, travel, and work. And over these three and a half decades, a lot about the city has changed.

Giants, like Trans World Airlines, once based in Kansas City's Northland, fell and institutions like the hoary haberdashery Woolf Brothers folded.

The Comets and the Kings both came and went. So did Joe Montana, and Bo Jackson too.

NASCAR built a racetrack to the west, and Sprint, a new arena downtown. Brush Creek got a face lift and The Crossroads District, once vacant and forlorn, has been resuscitated.

But no change has pleased me more than the growth and maturity of this city's foodways, especially in the last half decade.

Not too long ago, The American Restaurant was at the top and a sea of corporate chain restaurants below with few options between, other than a handful of steakhouses, barbecue joints, and Town Topic casting its neon glow long into the night.

But now, we have before us a burgeoning, independent restaurant scene supported by a dedicated corps of local farmers and food producers. And with them, has arisen a growing class of educated eaters, mindful and discerning, and demanding of quality and value. This is good news.

In my relatively short career as a food writer, I've been known less for flattery and more for my honesty. So, despite the culinary growth and progress about which I boast, I won't be the first to tell you that Kansas City has arrived. It hasn't. And, I hope it never does, for the journey is always far more interesting than the destination, the cusp far more compelling than the break. But, I can confidently tell you that there has never been a more exciting time to be eating here than now.

Thankfully, Pete Dulin had the foresight to capture this moment in Kansas City's culinary history with the following collection of recipes from some of our city's finest, contemporary talent.

Some of them are professional chefs with restaurants. Others are professional cooks with catering or other food-related businesses. Together, they form a patchwork of flavors that represent Kansas City, here and now. Thank you, Pete, for serving as our city's culinary curator, for cheering and teaching, collecting and sharing. May these last bites be the beginning of a feast.

Bonjwing Lee is a food writer, photographer, and co-author of bluestem: The Cookbook. *He writes about food at ulteriorepicure.com.*

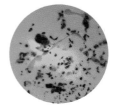

INTRODUCTION

A recipe is more than the sum of ingredients assembled and method followed until something edible results. A recipe may demystify the process of how a chocolate cake came to be, but it also represents something more than a paint-by-numbers approach to cooking.

The combination of ingredients and cooking techniques involved offer hints about the interplay of colors, flavors, textures, and aromas that make a summer salad or winter soup suitable for the season. History, geography, culture, and even memory can be enshrined in a recipe. Paying attention to those clues can yield more than a mouthful of food worth sharing. A recipe can connect us to another time and place and person, be it Julia Child or Rick Bayless or Aunt Betty and her version of potato salad.

My Thai mother Boonsom wrote down recipes in English, her newly adopted language, on index cards when she was learning how to cook midwestern dishes from my paternal grandmother Loretta. Yet, my mom has never recorded any of her Thai dishes in writing. I have emulated her process, but I'm still learning how to cook her dishes. I dread the day when she dies and I can never again taste her food the way she seasoned it. No recipe will duplicate her food. In other words, a recipe is a guide but it is not the dish itself.

The chefs and cooks I know, many of them represented in this book, have no qualms about sharing a recipe. Cooking takes time, patience, technique, and an understanding of ingredients based on the season, kitchen, equipment, and other factors to make adjustments. Thankfully, forty chefs and cooks have shared 100 recipes in *Last Bite* to give us a head start.

These cooks and chefs have different touchstones when it comes to food. Their recipes reflect a focus on farm-to-table cooking and seasonal dining as well as dietary concerns such as gluten-free foods. While the diversity of recipes in this book will appeal to many interests, the primary emphasis is simplicity. These eclectic recipes are simple in preparation and plating so you can get to the good part - eating and sharing with others. Try these recipes and have fun experimenting to make them your own.

Last Bite is a one-of-a-kind cookbook that represents only some of Kansas City's best culinary talent. It is a tribute to the people more than our city's food scene or reputation. Prepare and sample their dishes. Support their local business.

Experience each bite as if it were your last. Here's to good eating. To those already at the table, save us a seat.

Pete Dulin

Blue Crab & Avocado Cocktail

CHEF/OWNER JOHN WESTERHAUS, WESTCHASE GRILL

Chef Westerhaus shares this light and refreshing seafood recipe with a classy presentation.

Place six martini glasses in the refrigerator to chill. Drain 1 pound of lump blue crab meat. Gently check for pieces of shell or cartilage and discard.

In a small bowl, combine juice from 3 limes with flesh from 2 diced ripe avocados. In a medium-size bowl, combine crab meat, 1 medium diced tomato (reserve 1/2 cup for garnish), 2 medium diced shallots,

1 tablespoon coarsely chopped cilantro, and 3/4 cup mayonnaise. Gently fold ingredients until just mixed together to avoid breaking up crabmeat. Gently fold lime juice and avocado into mixture until combined.

Place 2-3 tablespoons shredded or thinly sliced romaine lettuce in bottom of each martini glass. Add equal parts of crab mixture to glasses. Garnish with reserved diced tomato, a sprig of cilantro and a lime wedge.

WestChase Grill is at 11942 Roe Avenue, Overland Park, KS westchasegrill.com.

Brewpub Cheese and Charcuterie

JUDITH FERTIG, BBQ QUEENS

"Planking with a little wood smoke makes grocery store deli meats and cheeses irresistible," says Fertig. "Layer small slices like capicola, salami or other sliced deli meat; roll larger cuts like prosciutto into cigars. The more surface of the meat or cheese that touches the plank, the more aromatic wood flavor you get in the food."

Use two cedar grilling or one baking plank, soaked in water for at least 1 hour. Prepare an indirect fire in the grill with a hot fire on one side and no fire on the other. Arrange cheese and meats separately on the plank(s) such as 1 (6-ounce) wedge blue cheese, 1 (6-ounce) wedge Fontina cheese, and 1 (6-ounce) wedge Gouda cheese. Add 16 slices coppa layered like shingles.

Scatter ½ cup hardwood chips (mesquite, hickory, oak) on the charcoal or in a foil packet poked with holes near a gas burner on a gas grill. Once smoking begins, place the plank(s) on the indirect heat side of the grill and close the lid. Grill for 15-20 minutes, or until cheese is burnished, aromatic, and has started to slightly melt. Serve right on the plank.

Recipe adapted from Heartland: The Cookbook *by Judith Fertig. Reprinted with permission of Andrews McMeel Publishing, LLC. BBQ Queens; bbqqueens.com.*

Caramelized Tomato Jam

CHEF GRANT WAGNER, JJ'S RESTAURANT

Chef Wagner uses tomato jam, made from locally grown heirloom tomatoes, with puff pastries, game meat, hearty fish, and even on toast for breakfast. Any tomatoes, homegrown or out of a can, will work. For this recipe you'll need 4 cups of tomatoes total.

In a heavy-bottomed pot, combine 2 cups sugar, a 4-inch cinnamon stick, 1 sprig of thyme, 1/4 cup tomato juice, 1 bay leaf, 2 whole pieces of star anise, 1 teaspoon ground allspice, juice from 2 lemons, and a pinch of salt. Place over medium-low heat. Stir until first liquefied and then slightly browned.

Puree 1 1/2 16-ounce cans whole, peeled tomatoes (or 3 cups fresh tomatoes), then stir into sugar mixture. Add remaining half can of tomatoes (or 1 cup fresh tomatoes). Add enough water to 2 tablespoons cornstarch to liquefy it. Stir into tomato jam. Bring to a boil, then reduce heat and simmer until thickened, about 7 minutes, stirring constantly. Remove cinnamon stick, thyme, bay leaf, and star anise. Cool and store covered for up to 6 months in refrigerator.

JJ's is at 910 W. 48th Street,
Kansas City, MO;
jjs-restaurant.com.

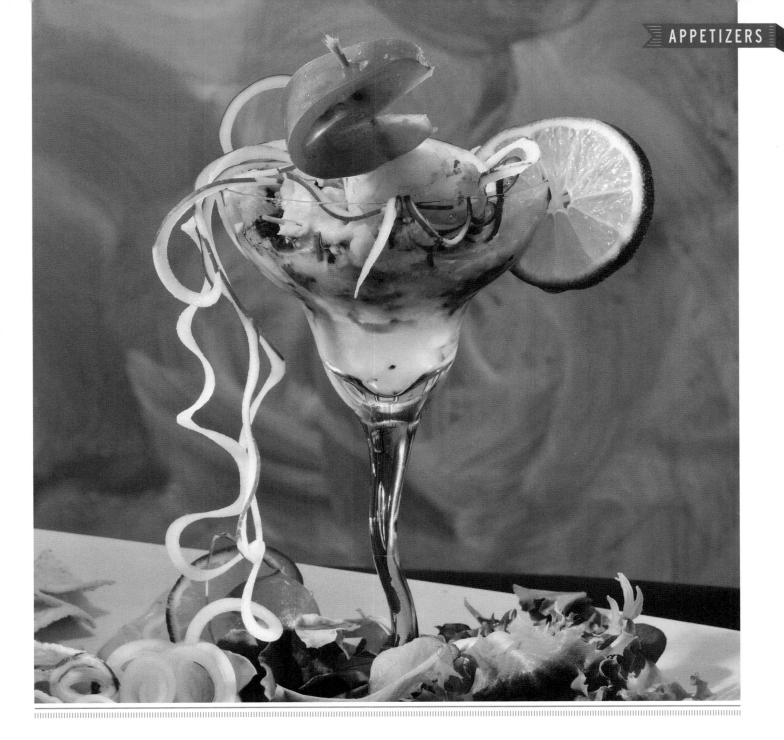

Ceviche

CHEF/OWNER BASILIO DE DIOS, LATIN BISTRO

This seafood ceviche from Chef Dios (aka Chef Tito) is ideal for a light meal in warm weather. Acidity from the lime and tomato "cooks" the seafood and infuses it with zesty flavor.

Using clean knives and cutting boards, chop 1 pound raw shrimp (deveined, with shell and tails removed) and 1 or 2 medium fillets of raw fish (such as tilapia) into bite-size pieces. Add salt and pepper to taste. Add juice from 2-3 fresh limes. Marinate mixture 8 hours or overnight in a tightly sealed container in the refrigerator.

After marinating or "cooking," finely chop 1 whole red or white onion, 2 medium tomatoes, 1 or 2 jalapeno peppers, 1 bunch of rinsed cilantro, and 1 peeled mango. Add to fish and shrimp. Chill for 1 hour. Serve with tortilla chips.

Latin Bistro is at 6924 North Oak Trafficway, Gladstone, MO; latinbistrokc.com.

Chilaquiles

CHEF/OWNER PATRICK RYAN, PORT FONDA

Chef Ryan's recipe for chilaquiles, a truly authentic Mexican food not usually found on local restaurant menus, is simple to prepare. Chilaquiles are often served for breakfast or brunch.

Cook 1/2 cup chorizo, a spicy Mexican sausage, until done. Drain excess grease. In a very lightly oiled skillet, sauté 2 cups tortilla chips over medium-high heat. Add cooked chorizo and 2 cups salsa. Cook until chips are soft and all ingredients are hot. Add water as needed if too dry. Garnish with sour cream, cilantro, and chopped onion.

Traditionally, a fried egg is served on top of the chilaquiles, Ryan says. Cooked, shredded chicken can be substituted for the chorizo.

Port Fonda is at 4141 Pennsylvania, Kansas City, MO; portfondakc.com.

Crawfish and Egg Bruschetta

CHEF JOHN MCCLURE, FORMER OWNER OF STARKER'S RESTAURANT

This brunch dish from Chef McClure drew inspiration from New Orleans, where he once worked. Several of his dishes paid homage to the bayou culture.

Remove crusts from 4 (3/4-inch-thick) slices of brioche Pullman bread (or favorite bread) and cut slices diagonally. Toast bread in nonstick pan with 1 tablespoon unsalted butter until golden and crisp. Set aside.

Cook 4 thin strips of La Quercia Tamworth bacon in pan over medium heat until crisp. (Substitute slices of regular bacon or pancetta, if desired.) Delicately remove bacon and set aside to drain grease.

Add 1/8 teaspoon minced garlic and 1 tablespoon finely diced shallots to a pan lightly coated with bacon grease. Sauté 1 minute until shallots have softened, but do not brown. Add 4 ounces crawfish tail meat and heat for 1 minute. Season with 1/4 teaspoon Paul Prudhomme's Seafood Magic seasoning blend and 1/4 teaspoon hot sauce. Whisk together 2 large eggs and 1 tablespoon crème fraîche and add to crawfish. Scramble eggs until they begin to set but remain creamy. Add 2 tablespoons thin-sliced chives.

On a plate, layer crawfish and egg topping on slice of brioche. Place a slice of bacon on eggs. Add slice of brioche on the side. Serves four.

Starker's Restaurant is at 201 West 47th Street, Kansas City, MO; starkersrestaurant.com.

Datiles con Pancetta (Dates With Pancetta)

OWNER JAMES TAYLOR, LA BODEGA

La Bodega celebrates the culinary and social tradition of Spanish tapas at its West Side location and in Leawood. By nature, tapas are meant to be enjoyed while socializing. While this recipe serves two, multiply as desired for more guests.

To prepare fig sauce, put 1 pound dry black mission figs, stems removed, in a pot with 1 cup orange juice, 3 cups water, 2 1/2 cups sugar and 1/4 teaspoon salt. Simmer on high heat until liquid reduces by 25 percent. Remove pot from heat, let sauce cool, and transfer to blender. Blend sauce until smooth and refrigerate until cold.

Make a slit down the side of 10 dates and remove the pit. Stuff each date with about half a teaspoon uncooked ground pork chorizo. Wrap a slice of pancetta around each stuffed date.

To cook dates, preheat oven to 350 degrees. Heat 1 ounce olive oil in a skillet over medium-high heat. Sauté dates for one minute. Transfer dates to an ovenproof dish and bake for 10 minutes or until pancetta is crispy and chorizo is cooked through. Serve with sauce on the side or under the dates. Garnish with chopped parsley.

La Bodega is at 703 Southwest Boulevard, Kansas City, MO, and 4311 West 119th Street, Leawood, KS; labodegakc.com.

Duck Empanadas

CHEF/CO-OWNER CARL THORNE-THOMSEN, STORY

Chef Thorne-Thomsen uses duck for this savory version of empanadas, a stuffed pastry found throughout Spain and Latin America. Look for duck meat at McGonigle's or the frozen section of the supermarket meat department.

Prepare empanada dough by mixing 1 cup all-purpose flour, 1/4 cup canola oil, 1/2 teaspoon salt, and 2 ounces water in a bowl. Knead gently and briefly until dough forms a smooth ball. Refrigerate one hour.

Finely dice 2 pounds of duck leg or breast meat. Brown meat in a large hot sauté pan, seasoning with salt and pepper to taste. Add 1 small minced yellow onion, 1 peeled and shredded carrot, 2 cloves minced garlic, and 1 tablespoon tomato paste. Cook 4-5 minutes.

Add 2 cups duck or chicken stock, 1 tablespoon lemon juice, 1 teaspoon fresh thyme, and additional salt and pepper. Cover pan, lower heat, and simmer for 30 minutes.

Divide dough into 3-4 pieces and roll into thin sheets. Using a 3-inch ring cutter, stamp circles out of the dough. Place a teaspoon of duck mixture in each circle and fold into a half moon. Pour 1/4 cup canola oil in a deep pan, heat medium-high (350 degrees), and fry empanadas until light brown in color. Serve with guacamole or sauce of your choice.

Story is at 3931 West 69th Terrace, Prairie Village, KS; storykc.com.

Fondue

CHEF JUSTIN VOLDAN, 12 BALTIMORE AT HOTEL PHILLIPS

Chef Voldan blends kirsch, a cherry brandy, with aromatic nutmeg and rosemary to introduce multi-layered flavor in this classic cheese dip. The kirsch may be omitted or, as a substitute, try using an equivalent amount of Leinenkugel Berry Weiss or Sam Adams Cherry Wheat beer.

Rub the inside of a large saucepan with a peeled clove of garlic. Heat 1 1/4 cups dry white wine and 1 teaspoon lemon juice until simmering but not boiling. In a bowl, toss 1 pound shaved or sliced Gruyere cheese and 6 ounces shaved or sliced Emmentaler cheese with 4 teaspoons flour.

Slowly add to wine in pan. Whisk continuously. Once all cheese is melted, add 1/4 teaspoon nutmeg, 1/4 teaspoon fresh or dried rosemary, and 1 tablespoon kirsch. If mixture is not thick enough, add more flour. If too thick, add more wine.

Serve with cubes of French bread for dipping.

12 Baltimore at Hotel Phillips is at 106 West 12th Street, Kansas City, MO; hotelphillips.com.

Heirloom Tomato Tart

CHEF JOHN MCCLURE, FORMER OWNER OF STARKER'S RESTAURANT

Toe-may-toe, toe-mah-toe. No matter how you pronounce it, heirloom tomatoes are summer's way of saying delicious. Chef McClure marries tomato and basil with goat cheese and puff pastry for pizzazz.

Defrost 1 sheet of frozen puff pastry for several minutes at room temperature. Cut the pastry into four 4-inch squares. Poke holes in center of the dough with a fork, leaving half-inch outer border of the dough untouched. Spread 1 tablespoon of basil pesto (homemade or prepared) onto the center of each dough square. Cut 2 heirloom tomatoes into slices, then cut slices in half and arrange equally on top. Crumble fresh goat cheese on top of tomatoes and season with salt and pepper. Drizzle tart with extra virgin olive oil. Bake in preheated 400-degree oven for about 30 minutes, or until golden brown.

The tarts make a great summertime appetizer, or serve two per person for a lunch entrée.

Starker's Restaurant is at 201 West 47th Street, Kansas City, MO; starkersrestaurant.com.

Parmesan and Cheddar Cheese Board with Grilled Grapes

KAREN ADLER AND JUDITH FERTIG, BBQ QUEENS

Adler and Fertig use wood grilling planks as a cooking surface. "Hard cheeses like Parmesan and Romano are very easy to plank," says Adler. "They pick up a lovely hint of wood aroma."

Soak a cedar or oak grilling plank in water for 1 hour. Prepare an indirect fire in the grill with a medium-hot fire on one side and no fire on the other. Brush 1 pound each of seedless green grapes and red grapes with 2 tablespoons of olive oil. Set aside. Place an 8-ounce wedge Parmesan or Romano cheese and an 8-ounce wedge cheddar cheese flat on grilling plank. The largest side of the wedges should rest on the plank.

Place plank on no-heat side of the grill and close lid. Cook for 15-20 minutes, or until cheddar cheese begins to ooze. Remove plank and grill grapes directly on medium-hot side of the grill, turning often, until grapes are scorched and blistered, about 4 minutes total. Arrange grapes beside the cheeses on a serving platter and serve with a basket of baguette slices.

Oven-Planking: Preheat the oven to 325°F. Place the planked cheese in the middle of the oven and oven-plank for 15 minutes, or until the cheddar cheese is beginning to ooze. Serve with fresh (uncooked) grapes and bread.

Recipe from 25 Essential Techniques for Planking *by Karen Adler & Judith Fertig (Harvard Common Press). Reprinted with permission. BBQ Queens; bbqqueens.com.*

Pimento Cheese Spread

CHEF/CO-OWNER NATHAN FELDMILLER, CAFÉ EUROPA

Chef Feldmiller says old-fashioned pimento spread on bread is a tasty, inexpensive snack when friends come over. "It's a fun thing to do that's easy to make with regular stuff you have lying around."

Feldmiller's version is a family recipe but not from his mom. "My mom was opposed to it, but my grandma liked to make it."

Toss about a cup of any firm cheeses you have left over from other things—cheddar or Jack are fine—into a food processor. Add a squirt of mustard and some fresh minced garlic or a pinch of garlic powder. Add mayonnaise and process until the mixture is spreadable. With a spatula, fold in a small jar of pimentos, add salt and pepper to taste, and spread on white bread.

Café Europa is at 323 East 55th Street, Kansas City, MO; cafeeuropakc.com.

Super Savory Cheese Ball

CRAIG JONES, SAVORY ADDICTIONS GOURMET NUTS

Try preparing this cheese ball for your Super Bowl party or any gathering where cheese is given due respect. Jones makes "small-batch artisan nuts" that are seasoned and smoked over wood.

Place these ingredients in a food processor and blend for one minute, scraping down sides as needed: 8 ounces softened cream cheese, 1 cup shredded, smoked gouda, 1 cup gorgonzola, 2 tablespoons mayonnaise, 1 tablespoon port wine, and 1 teaspoon minced garlic.

Shape cheese mixture into a ball, place in middle of a sheet of plastic wrap, wrap and refrigerate for 3 hours until firm. Unwrap cheese ball and roll it onto 1/2 cup coarsely chopped mixed nuts until fully covered. (Jones, of course, recommends his company's gourmet nuts.) Serve with crackers or bread. Optional: Add 1 tablespoon of your favorite barbecue sauce.

Kansas City area retailers for Savory Addictions Gourmet Nuts are available at savoryaddictions.com.

Autumn Vegetable Stew

JAMIE MILKS, EVERYDAY ORGANIC COOKERY

Milks uses seasonal vegetables to heighten the flavor of this hearty stew.

Preheat oven to 300 degrees. Line 2 baking sheets with paper towels. Peel and dice 2 small eggplants and 2 medium zucchini (4 cups each). Spread vegetables on baking sheets in a single layer, sprinkle with 2 teaspoons kosher salt and let sit for 30 minutes.

Heat 2 cups olive oil over medium heat in a 6-8 quart heavy-bottomed pot. Add 1 small diced onion and 4 stalks diced celery. Cook vegetables until they begin to soften. Add 1/4 cup minced garlic, 4 sprigs fresh oregano, and 1 bay leaf. Cook 3-4 minutes, stirring occasionally.

Pat zucchini and eggplant dry and add them to the pot. Toss everything in olive oil until evenly coated.

Cover and place pot in oven for 40 minutes or until vegetables are soft but not mushy. Gently turn vegetables several times while cooking. Remove pot from oven and drain off olive oil (reserve for another pot of stew). Add 2 cups cooked garbanzo beans, 1 cup cherry tomatoes sliced in half, and 4 cups water (or vegetable stock) to pot. Simmer 5-10 minutes. Salt and pepper to taste and serve with shaved Parmigiano Reggiano.

Everyday Organic Cookery; everydayorganiccookery.com

Black Bean Soup and Black Pepper Brie Sandwich

CHEF CHARLES D'ABLAING, CHAZ ON THE PLAZA

After a busy day of cooking at Chaz on the Plaza, Chef Charles d'Ablaing turns to this simple dish of black bean soup and a black pepper brie sandwich for sustenance at home.

In a pot, he heats two cans of black beans, a handful each of chopped carrots, onion and celery, two cups of chicken broth, and three cloves of garlic. Season the soup with a teaspoon of chili powder and a half-teaspoon of cumin. When the carrots are tender, pour the soup into a food processor and puree until smooth. Add salt and pepper to taste. Garnish with a sprinkle of sliced baby bok choy leaves or cilantro and a drizzle of sour cream. Serves four.

For a heartier meal, d'Ablaing places slices of brie, warmed to room temperature, on toasted bread and dusts them with cracked black pepper.

Chaz on the Plaza is at 325 Ward Parkway, Kansas City, MO; chazontheplaza.com.

Butternut Squash Bisque

CHEF/CO-OWNER CARL THORNE-THOMSEN, STORY

Chef Thorne-Thomsen turns to butternut squash for this creamy soup, perfect for frosty nights.

Use a sharp knife for easier preparation. Peel, remove seeds, and roughly chop 2 pounds butternut squash. Peel and roughly chop 1/2 pound sweet potato and 1 carrot. Chop 1 celery stalk, slice 1 yellow onion, and dice 1/4 cup apple. Add these ingredients to a medium saucepan with 2 fresh sage leaves, 3 sprigs fresh thyme, 2 cloves, 6-8 peppercorns, 1 tablespoon brown sugar and 1 teaspoon kosher salt.

Add just enough water to cover.

Bring to low boil and cook gently for 30 minutes or until all ingredients are soft. Puree in a blender, then pour through a sieve. Return to a clean saucepan, add 1 cup heavy cream and heat gently to just below a boil. Season with more salt if necessary. Serve in warm bowls and garnish with crumbled bacon and chopped parsley.

Story is at 3931 West 69th Terrace, Prairie Village, KS; storykc.com.

Chilled Cucumber and Yogurt Soup

CHEF/CO-OWNER NATHAN FELDMILLER, CAFÉ EUROPA

This recipe from Chef Feldmiller is perfect for combating oppressive summer heat. "I generally peel half the cucumbers so it has a nice pastel green color," he says.

Scoop the seeds out of 2 cucumbers, rough-chop the cucumber and add to a blender with 1 cup plain yogurt, salt and pepper to taste, and the juice of 1 lemon. Barely cover with cold water and blend. Chill until ready to serve.

Café Europa is at 323 East 55th Street, Kansas City, MO; cafeeuropakc.com.

Creamy Corn Soup with Goat Cheese

CHEF DEBBIE GOLD, THE AMERICAN RESTAURANT

It doesn't get much simpler than this one-ingredient recipe from Chef Gold.

To make soup for 4 people, shuck 12 ears of corn. Grate 8 of the ears into a bowl. Press the grated corn through a fine sieve; reserve the "milk" and discard the grated corn and the cobs. Cut kernels from the remaining 4 ears.

Combine the cut kernels and 1/2 cup of water in a medium pan over medium heat. Add salt and pepper to taste. Cover pan, stirring once or twice, until the corn is tender, about 5 minutes. Set the corn aside.

In a medium saucepan, stirring constantly, bring the corn milk to a simmer. Reduce heat to medium low and continue to stir until the milk thickens, about 3 minutes. Add the cooked corn, salt, and pepper. Cook until the corn is heated through. Serve warm.

If you like, garnish with crumbled goat cheese, chopped purple olives and chopped fresh chives.

The American Restaurant is at 2511 Grand Boulevard, Kansas City, MO; theamericankc.com.

Cucumber Avocado Bisque

SHERI PARR, THE BRICK

Bisque traditionally refers to a soup broth made from crustaceans, but it also includes cream-based soups. This soothing chilled soup from Parr is seafood-free and an easy way for landlubbers to foil sweltering summer weather.

Put the following ingredients in a blender and process until smooth: 1 avocado, pitted and peeled; 1 large cucumber, peeled and seeded; 1 cup plain yogurt; 1 cup chicken broth; 3 chopped green onions; 2 tablespoons lemon juice; and 1/4 teaspoon salt. Pour soup in a large bowl, cover and chill until ready to serve. Makes 4 servings.

The Brick is at 1727 McGee, Kansas City, MO; thebrickkcmo.com.

Gazpacho

SHERI PARR, THE BRICK

Summer is a prime time to prepare gazpacho, a refreshing cold soup with origins in Spain. Parr's recipe offers a cool lunch option for hot days. Use ripe tomatoes for maximum flavor. Heirloom tomatoes are a good bet.

Dice 4 medium tomatoes. Mince 1 medium onion, 1 red and 1 green bell pepper, and 1 peeled medium cucumber. All ingredients should be diced the same size. Combine in a large bowl with 2 tablespoons of red wine vinegar, 2 tablespoons of olive oil, 1 clove of garlic crushed, 2 cups of vegetable or tomato juice, a pinch of cumin powder, and salt and pepper to taste. Chill for two hours. Top the gazpacho with tortilla strips before serving.

The Brick is at 1727 McGee, Kansas City, MO;
thebrickkcmo.com

Italian-Style White Bean Soup

DUANE DAUGHERTY, MR. DOGGITY FOODS

"This soup is similar to an Italian wedding soup, but beans are a healthier alternative to pasta," says Duane Daugherty, the "barbeconnoisseur" behind locally made Mr. Doggity's BBQ Sauce.

Prepare meatballs by combining 1 pound ground turkey or chicken with 1 egg white, 1/2 cup seasoned Italian bread crumbs, salt and pepper. Shape into 1-inch-diameter meatballs. In a stockpot, heat 2 tablespoons extra-virgin olive oil over medium-high heat. Add meatballs and season with a dash of salt and pepper. Turn meatballs until brown on all sides (3-4 minutes total). Drain excess liquid. Add 1 finely chopped medium onion and sauté 4 minutes until translucent. Add 4-5 minced garlic cloves and cook 1 minute.

Add 1 (15.5 ounce) can cannellini or other white beans, drained and rinsed; 1 teaspoon each fresh chopped thyme and rosemary (or 1/2 teaspoon each of dried), 1 pinch red pepper flakes and 4 cups chicken broth. Bring to boil. Reduce heat, cover and simmer 5 minutes.

Wash and coarsely chop 1-2 cups fresh spinach, add to soup and simmer 5 more minutes. Adjust seasonings to taste.

Garnish with shredded Parmesan or Romano cheese and serve with crusty bread. Makes 4-6 servings.

Mr. Doggity Foods; mrdoggity.com.

Mushroom Soup

CHEF CHARLES D'ABLAING, CHAZ ON THE PLAZA

For a fancy touch, Chef d'Ablaing likes to top off each bowl of this mushroom soup with a morel that has been poached and stuffed with blue crab.

In a large pot, heat 1/4 pound unsalted butter and add 1 cup chopped leeks and 1 cup diced yellow onion. Cook over low heat for 15 minutes or until the leeks begin to brown.

Add 2 cups rough-chopped shiitake mushrooms, caps only, and 2 cups rough-chopped crimini mushrooms to the pot. Cook mushrooms for 10 minutes or until browned and tender. Add 1/4 cup all-purpose flour and cook for 3 minutes, scraping the bottom of the pot regularly.

Add 4 cups chicken stock a little at a time, stirring until smooth between each addition. Then add 1 teaspoon chopped thyme, and salt and pepper to taste. Bring soup to a boil. Reduce heat and simmer for 15 minutes.

Remove from heat, puree soup, and add 2 cups heavy cream and 1/2 cup chopped fresh parsley. Before serving, season again with salt and pepper to taste, heat through but do not boil and add 1 cup dry sherry.

Chaz on the Plaza is at 325 Ward Parkway, Kansas City, MO; chazontheplaza.com.

Parmesan and Lentil Soup

CHEF/OWNER MICHAEL SMITH, EXTRA VIRGIN/MICHAEL SMITH

Chef Smith enhances the humble flavor of lentils with Parmesan cheese. He suggests serving this soup piping hot with a sprinkling of Parmesan and a drizzle of good-quality olive oil on top, plus garlic-Parmesan crostinis.

The Parmesan broth requires advance preparation time. Combine 4 ounces Parmesan cheese with 2 quarts water or chicken broth. Bring to a boil. Simmer for two hours. Strain the broth and reserve.

Peel and dice 1 yellow onion, 1 medium carrot, and 1 parsnip into 1/4-inch cubes. Add 4 tablespoons olive oil to a large pot and heat over high flame until the oil starts to smoke.

Add diced vegetables and cook 5-7 minutes until vegetables start to soften. Add 1 clove minced garlic and cook for 1 minute. Add 2 cups rinsed brown or green lentils, 2 bay leaves, 2 sprigs fresh thyme, and 1 teaspoon tomato paste. Stir for one minute. Add reserved Parmesan broth and bring to a boil.

Simmer slowly until lentils soften. Season with salt and pepper to taste, adding water as necessary. The lentils will absorb most of it as they cook. Take out bay leaves and thyme before serving.

The soup as shown here is garnished with a jicama-cucumber-tomato relish, parsley and homemade potato crisps.

Extra Virgin and Michael Smith is at 1900 Main Street, Kansas City, MO; extravirginkc.com, michaelsmithkc.com.

Smoked Ham Hocks and Black Bean Soup

CHEF/OWNER MICHAEL FOUST, THE FARMHOUSE

Smoking meat and other foods not only preserves the shelf life, it also imparts a flavor and aroma practically guaranteed to trigger hunger pangs. Chef Foust uses inexpensive ham hocks to add smoky, salty flavor to this hearty dish.

Soak 1 pound dry black beans overnight. Remove any impurities and drain. Medium-dice 1 onion, 1 bulb of fennel, 2 celery stalks, 2 peeled carrots, and 1 small peeled and de-seeded acorn squash. Set aside in a large bowl.

Heat large pot over medium-high heat. Brown 1 smoked ham hock and 6 slices medium-diced bacon in pot. Drain excess grease, if desired. Add vegetables and cook until onion is translucent. Add 4 tablespoons sherry vinegar and 1/2 cup red wine. Simmer until liquid is reduced by half.

Add 1 (16-ounce) can crushed tomatoes, the beans, 2 cloves diced garlic, 1 tablespoon dry oregano, and 4 cups chicken stock. Season with salt and pepper to taste. Cook until beans are tender, about 45 minutes.

The Farmhouse is at 300 Delaware Street, Kansas City, MO; eatatthefarmhouse.com.

Sweet Corn Soup with Crab

CHEFS COLBY AND MEGAN GARRELTS, OWNERS OF BLUESTEM

This recipe comes from Chefs Colby and Megan Garrelts, authors of *bluestem: The Cookbook.*

Rub 3 ears of corn, husks and silk removed, with 1 tablespoon extra-virgin olive oil. Season liberally with salt and pepper. Roast corn over grill or open flame of a gas stove, rotating ears until evenly charred. Once cool, cut kernels off corncobs. Working over a separate bowl, "milk" corn cobs by pressing the back of a knife down the length of the corn cobs. Reserve liquid and discard corn cobs.

In a medium-size pot, heat 1 tablespoon olive oil over medium-high heat. Add 2 large finely chopped shallots and 4 finely chopped garlic cloves and cook for 1 minute. Stir in corn and cook for another minute. Add 1 cup rye whisky, 1/2 cup dry white wine, and reserved corn milk. Season with salt and pepper to taste. Let mixture simmer for 5 minutes. Add 1 1/2 cups heavy cream. Return to a simmer and reduce soup for 10 minutes. Remove pot from heat and cool for 10 minutes.

Carefully pour hot mixture into a blender. With one hand held firmly over the lid, puree soup on high until smooth and liquefied, about 5 minutes. Strain soup through fine-mesh sieve or double-lined cheesecloth. Press pulp with flat spoon to yield as much liquid as possible.

Put 1 ounce jumbo lump crab meat in each of four bowls. Pour 1/4 cup hot soup into each bowl and garnish with a dash of freshly squeezed lime juice.

bluestem is at 900 Westport Road, Kansas City, MO; bluestemkc.com.

Tomato Tarragon Soup

CHEF JUSTIN VOLDAN, 12 BALTIMORE AT HOTEL PHILLIPS

Tarragon is often paired with chicken, fish, or eggs. Chef Voldan boosts the flavor and aroma of tomato soup with the distinctive herb also known as dragon's wort or little dragon.

Heat 1 tablespoon olive oil in a large pan over medium heat. Add 1 finely chopped small onion, 1 sliced celery stalk, 1/8 cup sliced carrot (2 tablespoons), and 1 minced garlic clove; cook for 2 minutes. Add 3 pounds fresh ripe tomatoes (stems removed), 2 tablespoons chopped fresh tarragon (or 1 1/2 teaspoons dried tarragon), and 2 cups low-sodium vegetable broth.

Simmer gently on low heat, uncovered, for 20 minutes.

Add 1 cup heavy cream. Use hand blender to puree soup until smooth. Add salt and pepper to taste and reheat to serving temperature. Garnish with sprigs of fresh tarragon. Serves 6.

12 Baltimore at Hotel Phillips is at 106 W. 12th St.; hotelphillips.com.

Apple Sage Walnut Salad

CHEF/OWNER MICHAEL FOUST, THE FARMHOUSE

Chef Foust recommends this salad as a side for pork dishes.

Slice 3 red apples with a julienne cut and discard cores. Mince 1 mild red chili pepper. Toast 1/4 cup black walnuts and break into medium-size pieces. Thinly slice 1/2 tablespoon fresh sage and a few small leaves of young mustard greens.

In a large bowl, toss apples, chili pepper, walnuts, sage, mustard greens, 2 tablespoons sherry vinegar, 1/2 teaspoon honey, and a dash of kosher salt. Mix all ingredients and adjust salt to taste before serving.

The Farmhouse is at 300 Delaware Street, Kansas City, MO; eatatthefarmhouse.com.

Asparagus and Arugula Salad

CHEF/OWNER RENÉE KELLY, RENÉE KELLY'S HARVEST

Chef Kelly serves this seasonal spring salad with lobster risotto. Try using asparagus from a local farm or farmers market when available.

Whisk together 1/4 cup rice wine vinegar, 1/2 cup safflower, grapeseed or light oil, and 1/2 teaspoon honey. Season the dressing with salt and pepper to taste.

"It should be lightly acidic with a mild sweetness, just enough to help break down the asparagus, but not overpowering," Kelly says. "All flavors of the arugula, asparagus, and radish should show through."

Toss 1 cup washed arugula and 6 asparagus spears (uncooked), sliced thin diagonally, in the dressing. Separate salad on two plates. Top with fresh radish shavings.

Renée Kelly's Harvest is at 12401 Johnson Drive, Shawnee Mission, KS; reneekellys.com.

Bacon Vinaigrette

CHEF ROBERT BRASSARD, BROADMOOR BISTRO

Bacon receives ample attention as an ingredient, but bacon fat, used in moderation, deserves its due. It adds concentrated flavor (here with a spinach salad), balanced by tangy vinegar, in this dressing. Chef Brassard suggests serving the vinaigrette warm or at room temperature.

Put 1/2 cup brown sugar, 1/2 tablespoon Dijon mustard, 1/8th chopped red onion, 1 peeled and chopped garlic clove, and 3/4 cup rice wine vinegar into a stainless steel pot. Bring to a simmer over medium heat. Reduce by at least half until syrupy.

Remove from heat and allow to cool slightly. Place mixture in blender; start on low speed and gradually increase. Slowly add 1/4 cup melted bacon fat and blend to emulsify. If mixture gets too thick, add a little water to thin out. Yields about 1 cup.

Broadmoor Bistro, a student-run culinary program at Broadmoor Technical Center in the Shawnee Mission School District, is at 6701 West 83rd Street, Overland Park, KS. The eatery is open during the school year; broadmoorbistro.org.

Betty Bailey Berry Salad

CHEF/CO-OWNER SANDI CORDER-CLOOTZ, EDEN ALLEY CAFÉ

Chef Corder-Clootz recommends this salad named for a customer who was also the head of a church women's auxiliary. "She was a feisty and strong lady, full of beauty," Corder-Clootz says. "This salad holds those qualities."

In a large salad bowl, layer the following ingredients: 8 cups mixed greens; 1/2 cup cooked couscous; two Granny Smith apples, sliced; 1/2 cup baby beets, peeled and cooked as desired; 1/2 cup mandarin oranges, segmented; 1/2 cup dried cranberries; a few slices of red onion; 1/4 cup candied walnuts; and 1/8 cup feta cheese (optional).

Top with your favorite poppy seed dressing. Serves four.

"The tartness of the crisp apples and dried cranberries is perfectly complemented by the sweetness of the mandarin oranges," Corder-Clootz says. The optional addition of feta cheese helps meld the flavors together, while the walnuts add a nice crunch. The addition of couscous transforms this salad into a hearty meal.

Eden Alley Café is at 707 West 47th Street, lower level of Unity Temple; edenalley.com.

Caramelized Cauliflower Salad

CHEF JOHN MCCLURE, FORMER OWNER OF STARKER'S RESTAURANT

Caramelization is a cooking process in which sugar turns brown when heat is applied. Chef McClure uses this technique and roasted pecans to add a sweet, nutty taste to this cauliflower salad.

Prepare dressing by whisking together 2 tablespoons whole grain Dijon mustard, 1 tablespoon creamy Dijon mustard, and 1 tablespoon red wine vinegar. Add 3 tablespoons extra-virgin olive oil and continue whisking until blended well.

In a sauté pan over high heat, add 2 tablespoons olive oil and 4 cups small cauliflower florets. Sauté cauliflower one minute without tossing until browning begins. Add 2 tablespoons butter and sauté another minute until cauliflower browns nicely. Add 2 ounces (about 4-5 slices) cooked thick-cut bacon diced roughly, 1/4 cup chopped roasted pecans, and 16 cloves roasted garlic. Turn off heat and add 1/2 cup of the vinaigrette.

Toss mixture and place in a mixing bowl. Add one Fuji apple, cut into matchsticks, and 1 cup flat leaf parsley. Season salad with salt and pepper to taste. Toss salad again and serve.

Starker's Restaurant is at 201 West 47th Street Kansas City, MO; starkersrestaurant.com.

Cucumber Salad

KEITH BUCHANAN, THE TEAHOUSE AND COFFEEPOT

Cucumbers originated in India centuries ago and were gradually cultivated in Asia, Western Europe, the Caribbean, and North America. The thin-skinned, semi-seedless English cucumber is one of hundreds of varieties. Buchanan uses the English cuke for this simple summer salad.

Wash and thinly slice 1 English cucumber. Sprinkle with salt, rub in, and let sit for 30 minutes on a plate or shallow bowl; the salt draws excess water out. Pour off salty liquid and add 2 tablespoons cider vinegar, 2 tablespoons sugar or honey, 1 teaspoon dill, and ground pepper to taste. Cover and let marinate in the refrigerator for 30 minutes or longer before serving.

The Teahouse and Coffeepot is at 4309 Jefferson Street, Kansas City, MO; teahousekc.com.

Frisee, Burrata, and Heirloom Tomato Summer Salad

CHEF/OWNER MICHAEL SMITH, EXTRA VIRGIN/MICHAEL SMITH

Burrata, an Italian word derived from "burro" or butter, is a fresh, rich cheese where the outer shell is solid mozzarella and the inside contains both mozzarella and cream. Chef Smith uses burrata with heirloom tomatoes and basil in a twist on the classic salad that typically uses fresh mozzarella (can be substituted for burrata).

Wash and slice 4 medium to large tomatoes in wedges, slices, or cubes to vary presentation. Season them generously with salt and pepper. Wash, dry, and cut off green tops of 2-3 heads frisee lettuce. Slice 1 ball of burrata into rounds.

On the center of four plates, alternate layers of tomatoes and frisee greens to build some height for the salad. Lay a burrata slice on top of salad. Season burrata with salt and pepper. Mix juice from one lemon and ¼ cup olive oil for dressing and drizzle over burrata and on the plates.

Serve with a good quality crusty bread. Serves 4.

Michael Smith Restaurant and Extra Virgin is at 1900 Main Street, Kansas City, MO; michaelsmithkc.com and extravirginkc.com.

Grilled Bread Salad With Spring Onions and Chipotle-Buttermilk Vinaigrette

CHEF/OWNER ALEX POPE, THE LOCAL PIG

Grilling bread adds a faint smoky flavor to this salad. Chipotle pepper enhances the smokiness and infuses subtle heat into the dressing. The tang of creamy buttermilk and herbal notes of rosemary round out the flavor profile.

Light the grill and bring to medium heat. Meanwhile, prepare vinaigrette by combining in a blender 1 cup buttermilk, 3 chipotle peppers (canned), 1/2 cup vegetable oil, 1 teaspoon salt and 1 teaspoon fresh rosemary leaves. Puree for 30 seconds and set aside.

Thinly slice 1 bunch green onions and place in large bowl. Brush canola oil on 1/4 -inch thick slices of 1 baguette. Place bread on grill and toast lightly, about 30 seconds per side. Add grilled bread to large bowl with onions and 2 cups arugula. Drizzle dressing on salad to taste, toss ingredients and serve.

The Local Pig is at 2618 Guinotte Avenue, Kansas City, MO; thelocalpig.com.

High Heat Grilled Romaine Salad

KAREN ADLER AND JUDITH FERTIG, BBQ QUEENS

Salad made with grilled lettuce? Believe it or not, it works. Adler and Fertig prepare this salad with a light, smoky flavor in mere minutes.

Prepare a hot fire on the grill. Cut lengthwise a head of romaine. Do not cut the core or the outer leaves will fall off. Rinse and dry well. Brush cut side of the lettuce with olive oil and grill cut side down for about 3 to 4 minutes, until you get good char marks. Leave the lid of the grill open while grilling. Grill lettuce on the cut side only and do not turn it. Serve with Caesar dressing of your choice and some freshly grated Parmesan cheese.

For a more substantial dish, add slices of grilled chicken breast to the salad.

Reprinted from The Gardener & The Grill by permission of RUNNING PRESS, a member of Perseus Books Group. BBQ Queens; bbqqueens.com.

Lime and Ginger Salmon Salad

CHEF/OWNER RENÉE KELLY, RENÉE KELLY'S HARVEST

This recipe from Chef Kelly combines tart lime, spicy ginger, cool cucumber, and peppery arugula to perk up a salmon salad.

Whisk together 2 tablespoons lime juice, 1 teaspoon finely grated ginger, and 3 teaspoons olive oil. Pour half the lime mixture over a 7-ounce salmon filet in a non-metallic bowl. Marinate for 10 minutes.

In a separate bowl, combine 1 1/2 cups fresh English or sugar snap peas, 2 thinly sliced green onions or garlic chives, 1/3 cup basil, 1 cup arugula, and 1 thinly sliced English cucumber.

Heat a nonstick frying pan over medium heat. Heat 1 tablespoon olive oil. Sprinkle salmon with sea salt, fresh cracked black pepper, and a pinch of ground coriander. Cook salmon in heated pan skin side down for 5 minutes, flip, and cook an additional 5 minutes. If desired, cook longer until done to preference. Remove skin and break filet into pieces. Combine with salad. Serve salad with remaining half of lime ginger vinaigrette. Serves 4.

Renée Kelly's Harvest is at 12401 Johnson Drive, Shawnee Mission, KS; reneekellys.com.

Louisiana Crawfish Salad

CHEF JOHN MCCLURE, FORMER OWNER OF STARKER'S RESTAURANT

Chef John McClure once lived in New Orleans, where he learned authentic Creole and Cajun cooking techniques. His recipe pays tribute to the cuisine with dishes inspired by the region.

Prepare vinaigrette by whisking together 1/4 cup chopped tarragon, 1 1/2 tablespoons Champagne vinegar, and 3 tablespoons extra-virgin olive oil. Set aside. Toss 1 bunch washed watercress leaves, 1/2 head thinly sliced fennel, 6 sliced radishes, and 4-6 sliced asparagus spears in a bowl with 3/4th of the vinaigrette. Season salad with salt and pepper to taste.

Place a portion of salad in the center of four plates. Toss 8 ounces of Louisiana crawfish tail meat with remaining vinaigrette, place on top of salad, and serve.

Crawfish tail meat can be shucked from whole crawfish available in the grocery store seafood section, or ask the seafood department to order crawfish meat. McGonigle's Market also carries frozen crawfish.

Starker's Restaurant is at 201 West 47th Street Kansas City, MO; starkersrestaurant.com.

Peach Salad With Creole Corn Fritters

CHEF JOHN MCCLURE, FORMER OWNER OF STARKER'S RESTAURANT

Chef McClure's dish balances different textures and flavors with a down-to-earth distillation of summer. The onions can be marinated a half-day ahead, but they can keep for two to three weeks in a sealed container in the refrigerator.

To prepare salad, cut 1 small peach per serving (or 1/2 large peach) into 8 wedges. Season with salt and black pepper. Grill peaches over high heat (gas or charcoal) just enough to mark them. Remove and drizzle with equal parts extra-virgin olive oil and sherry vinaigrette.

Slice 1 sweet onion and marinate in equal parts white vinegar and lemon-lime soda (up to 1 cup liquid, enough to coat onions). To prepare fritters, whisk 3 eggs in a bowl until frothy.

Add 1/2 cup milk and whisk until fully blended.

Sift together 1 cup flour, 1 tablespoon baking powder, 1 tablespoon sugar, and 1 teaspoon salt in a bowl; add to egg mixture and whisk until smooth. Fold in 2 cups cooked rice and 2 cups sweet corn kernels. Combine thoroughly. Heat deep fryer to 350 degrees or use deep pan with cooking oil on high heat. Fry spoonfuls, 1 1/2 tablespoons each, of batter for 3-4 minutes or until golden. Remove and drain.

Arrange each serving of peaches and onion on plates with fresh basil drizzled with olive oil. Serve with freshly fried fritters.

Starker's Restaurant is at 201 West 47th Street, Kansas City, MO; starkersrestaurant.com.

Pomegranate and Mixed Greens Salad

CHEF/CO-OWNER TED HABIGER, ROOM 39

This simple dish by Chef Habiger makes a pretty accompaniment to whatever is on your menu, especially for Valentine's Day.

"I often think of pomegranates around Valentine's Day," Habiger says. "You cut them open and all these seeds fall out and they pop in your mouth like caviar."

Put a package of baby mixed greens in a bowl and salt and pepper to taste. Add thinly sliced red onions if you like them and toss with dressing well before adding the final ingredients. Habiger makes a

vinaigrette of 1 part red wine vinegar to 3 parts extra virgin olive oil, but bottled red wine vinaigrette also works. Divide the lettuce onto serving plates.

For the finishing touches, grate some ricotta salata (salted ricotta cheese) from a gourmet grocery store on top, add some walnut halves and sprinkle the pomegranate seeds on top.

Room 39 is at 1719 West 39th Street, Kansas City, MO and 10561 Mission Road, Leawood, KS; rm39.com.

Roasted Beet Salad with Feta Cheese and Orange

CHEF/OWNER RENÉE KELLY, RENÉE KELLY'S HARVEST

"Beets provide a grounding energy to our diet," says Chef Kelly. Beets are high in fiber and good sources of beta carotene and vitamin C.

Heat oven to 400 degrees. Remove skin, tops and roots from 1 pound of beets. Wash beets, and then toss in a bowl with 1 tablespoon olive oil, 1 teaspoon salt, and 1/2 teaspoon black pepper. Pour beets into baking dish and roast for 40 minutes or until soft. Let cool, then slice into coins.

For dressing, whisk together 1 tablespoon orange juice, 1/4 cup olive oil, 1 tablespoon honey, and 1 tablespoon rice wine vinegar. Toss dressing with 1 pound washed watercress.

On four plates, layer salad starting with beet slices, then watercress, then repeat. Garnish salads with 4 ounces crumbled feta cheese, segments from one peeled orange and cracked black pepper. Serves four.

Renée Kelly's Harvest is at 12401 Johnson Drive, Shawnee Mission, KS; reneekellys.com.

Sunflower Sprouts and Asparagus Salad

SHERI PARR, THE BRICK

For this recipe, check for fresh asparagus at your local farmers market.

Trim and discard woody ends from 1 pound of asparagus. Place stalks in boiling water with 2 teaspoons salt and cook for 2 minutes or until slightly tender. Drain and rinse asparagus under cold water and set aside. Thinly slice 1/2 cup cucumber, 1 cup red bell pepper, and 1/2 cup radishes.

Make white wine vinaigrette by whisking together 1/3 cup white wine or Champagne vinegar, 1/4 cup fresh-squeezed lemon juice, 1 teaspoon honey, 1/4 teaspoon kosher salt, and 1/4 teaspoon black pepper in medium-sized bowl. Still whisking, slowly add 3/4 cup extra-virgin olive oil in a steady stream.

In a large bowl, combine 4 cups spring lettuce mix and 8 ounces sunflower sprouts (or substitute alfalfa sprouts). Add half of vinaigrette and toss carefully until coated. Divide salad among 4 plates.

Cover each salad with equal portions of asparagus, cucumber, red bell pepper, and radishes. Drizzle salads with a little more vinaigrette. Place 1 tablespoon goat cheese on each salad. Serve with remaining vinaigrette and a sprinkle of sea salt.

The Brick is at 1727 McGee, Kansas City, MO; thebrickkcmo.com.

Tomato and Watermelon Salad

CHEFS COLBY AND MEGAN GARRELTS, OWNERS OF BLUESTEM

In Kansas City, it's the heat and the humidity. It's a double whammy in summer. Light and juicy dishes like Chef Garrelts' tomato and watermelon salad can help us keep a cool head when hunger pangs strike.

Wash 1 cup of loose-packed wild arugula and 20 cherry-sized heirloom tomatoes. Cut the rind from one small seedless yellow watermelon. With a melon baller, preferably the size of the tomatoes, scoop out 20 balls from the melon. Place the watermelon balls, arugula, and tomatoes in a salad bowl. Add 2 ounces of balsamic vinegar and 1 ounce of extra virgin olive oil. Season the salad with sea salt and black pepper. That's the scoop! Serves 4.

Note: Heirloom tomatoes—more flavorful and colorful than hothouse and bulk tomatoes—have become more available in local grocery stores and farmers markets when in season.

bluestem is at 900 Westport Road, Kansas City, MO; bluestemkc.com.

Watermelon and Strawberry Salad

CHEF/OWNER MICHAEL SMITH, EXTRA VIRGIN/MICHAEL SMITH

Chef Smith uses feta cheese to add tang to this juicy summer salad.

For a single serving of this salad, use 6 pieces of watermelon cut into 1/2-inch squares. Toss watermelon in stainless steel bowl with 3 strawberries stemmed and quartered, 1 tablespoon feta cheese, 1 tablespoon extra-virgin olive oil, 1 teaspoon fresh-squeezed lemon juice and salt and pepper to taste. Mix well. Place the salad on plate and top with 1/3 cup baby salad greens or spring mix.

Michael Smith Restaurant and Extra Virgin is at 1900 Main Street, Kansas City, MO; michaelsmithkc.com and extravirginkc.com.

Arugula and Artichoke au Gratin

CHEF TATE AUSTIN ROBERTS, EBT

Chef Roberts offers a creative twist on spinach artichoke dip. He says, "It's perfect for family movie night at home or to take to your most formal holiday event."

Combine the following in a mixing bowl and toss by hand: 1/2 cup heavy cream; 6 ounces chopped arugula; 8 ounces canned, chopped artichokes; 1 tablespoon chopped garlic; 12 ounces cream cheese; 2 tablespoons brown sugar; 1 tablespoon kosher salt; a pinch of cayenne pepper; and the juice from 3 lemons.

Do not use a food processor. This needs to be chunky, Roberts says.

Pour mixture in a 9-inch cake pan or a medium-sized ovenproof skillet and top with 2 cups Italian bread crumbs and 1/4 cup olive oil. Bake at 425 degrees for 12 minutes. Remove, sprinkle grated Parmesan cheese on top, and let stand five minutes.

Serve with pita chips cut into wedges, tossed with chopped garlic and olive oil, and toasted in oven at 350 degrees for 10 minutes. Toasted pita chips are available at most stores as well.

EBT Restaurant is at 1310 Carondelet Drive #100, Kansas City, MO; ebtrestaurant.com.

Brussels Sprouts With Almonds

CHEF LEON BAHLMANN, CAFE TRIO

"This simple vegetarian Brussels sprouts recipe uses toasted almonds instead of the pork that many recipes call for in food pairings," says Chef Bahlmann.

Trim stems off 1 pound of Brussels sprouts. Using a knife, score bottoms of stems with an X. Bring 4 cups salted water in a large pot to a boil, then cook sprouts about 5 minutes. Remove sprouts from water, place in a bowl of water and ice until completely chilled, and drain. Cut in half through stem and set aside.

In a large pan, lightly sauté 2 tablespoons chopped garlic and 1 cup sliced red onion in 2 tablespoons olive oil for 2 minutes. Add sprouts and sauté over medium-high heat until lightly browned, about 3 minutes. Add 1/4 cup chopped dried apricots, 2 tablespoons fresh lemon juice, and salt and pepper to taste. Toss until warm and blended. Garnish dish with 1/2 cup sliced or slivered toasted almonds. Serves 4.

Cafe Trio is at 4558 Main Street, Kansas City, MO; cafetriokc.com.

Confetti Coleslaw

DUANE DAUGHERTY, MR. DOGGITY FOODS

"When I cater a barbecue event, I always serve confetti coleslaw," says Daugherty of Mr. Doggity Foods, which makes and sells barbecue sauce, caters, and offers classes on smoking, grilling, and sausage-making.

"This coleslaw has become my 83-year-old mother-in-law's 'go-to' dish for those last minute church potlucks, receptions and funerals in her small town. She, too, nearly always gets asked for the recipe."

Shred one small green cabbage head along with 2-3 peeled carrots in a large bowl. Add 1/4 cup total of diced red, yellow and/or orange bell pepper; 1/4 cup diced green pepper; and 1/4 cup diced sweet onion.

Stir 1/4 cup sugar into the mixture. (Daugherty's mother-in-law often uses a sugar substitute such as Splenda.)

For dressing, combine in a bowl 1/3 cup vegetable oil, 1/2 cup vinegar, 2 teaspoons kosher salt, and 2 teaspoons celery seed. Pour into saucepan and bring to a boil. Pour over coleslaw, stir, and chill at least one hour. Drain off excess liquid before serving.

Mr. Doggity Foods; mrdoggity.com.

Creamy Coleslaw

CHEF/OWNER RENÉE KELLY, RENÉE KELLY'S HARVEST

Chef Kelly uses apple cider vinegar in this creamy coleslaw recipe. "Vinegar is a flavor enhancer, preservative, and digestive aid," Kelly says. "The best apple cider vinegar is cloudy when it still contains the 'mother,' a mixture containing active enzymes and beneficial bacteria."

Whisk together 2 tablespoons apple cider vinegar, 1 cup plain yogurt, and 1 tablespoon honey in a small bowl. In a large bowl, toss together 1 tablespoon chopped cilantro, 1 teaspoon chopped mint, 1/2 cup thin-sliced shallots, 2 pounds thin-sliced green cabbage, and 1 cup shredded carrots.

Pour yogurt mixture over cabbage mixture and coat thoroughly. Season slaw with 1/4 teaspoon ground coriander. Add a pinch of salt and pepper to taste. Serves 8.

Renée Kelly's Harvest is at 12401 Johnson Drive, Shawnee Mission, KS; reneekellys.com.

Granny Smith Applesauce

CHEF BRIAN AARON, TANNIN WINE BAR AND KITCHEN

"This applesauce pairs well with roast chicken, duck or pork tenderloin," says Chef Aaron.

Peel 8 Granny Smith apples and dice into small cubes. Meanwhile, in a large saucepan, combine 1/2 cup local honey, 1/2 cup sugar, 1/2 cup spiced rum, 1 teaspoon cinnamon, and 1/4 teaspoon each ground cardamom, allspice, and nutmeg. Simmer over medium heat 3-4 minutes.

Add diced apples to saucepan and stir until apples become tender

about 5 minutes. Cool mixture slightly. Use a food processor to puree half of the cooked apples, taking care that the warm apple puree doesn't splatter. Combine both mixtures and refrigerate before serving. The applesauce (shown here served with a potato latke) can also be served warm.

Tannin Wine Bar and Kitchen is at 1526 Walnut Street, Kansas City, MO; tanninwinebar.com.

Green Asparagus With Black Olive Tapenade, Almonds, and Goat Cheese

CHEF DEBBIE GOLD, THE AMERICAN RESTAURANT

Chef Gold suggests this recipe for spring when fresh asparagus is in season. The recipe calls for black olive tapenade that can be prepared using recipes online or purchased at a grocery store.

Using 2 bunches of green asparagus, hold spears individually by the tip and base and bend each until it snaps. Discard ends that are hard and woody. Heat 3 tablespoons olive oil in a large sauté pan. Cook asparagus over medium heat for about 10 minutes, stirring often.

When asparagus is tender, add 4 tablespoons black olive tapenade and a light touch of salt and freshly ground black pepper to taste. (Keep in mind that tapenade is already salty.) Toss until asparagus is well-coated.

Place asparagus on serving platter with tips facing the same direction. Sprinkle 4 ounces crumbled fresh goat cheese and 1/4 cup whole almonds, toasted and coarsely chopped, on top of asparagus.

The American Restaurant is located at 2511 Grand Boulevard, Kansas City, MO; theamericankc.com.

Potato Latkes

CHEF BRIAN AARON, TANNIN WINE BAR AND KITCHEN

Chef Aaron serves potato latkes with pan-roasted foie gras, but they also pair well with roast chicken or duck.

In a large mixing bowl, grate 4 scrubbed (but not peeled) russet potatoes and 1/2 medium yellow onion using largest holes on a hand grater. Add 2 tablespoons each chopped fresh parsley, thyme, and chives; 4 eggs; 2 cups matzo meal or panko bread crumbs; 1 tablespoon kosher salt; and 1 tablespoon lemon juice. Combine, cover mixture, and refrigerate for 1 hour.

Heat large nonstick skillet on medium-high heat. Add enough olive oil to cover bottom of pan. When oil just begins to smoke, carefully drop batter in 3-inch circles or desired size. Brown pancakes 1-2 minutes on each side, allowing edges to crisp and center to cook fully.

Transfer latkes to tray lined with paper towels. Serve with applesauce and honey, or sour cream with ground cinnamon seasoned to taste. Serves 8.

Tannin Wine Bar and Kitchen is at 1526 Walnut Street, Kansas City, MO; tanninwinebar.com.

Quick Pickled Beets

CHEF/OWNER RENÉE KELLY, RENÉE KELLY'S HARVEST

Chef Kelly gives her pickled beets extra zip with the use of star anise, hot pepper, and orange zest. Served chilled, these beets look lively and colorful on the table at potlucks and picnics.

Peel and cut 1 pound of beets into 1/8th-inch slices. Place slices into a large pot with 1 tablespoon kosher salt, 1 cup rice wine vinegar, 1 cup water, 1/2 cup granulated sugar, 1 teaspoon orange zest, 1 teaspoon hot pepper (seeded and diced), 1/4 cup diced onion, and 1 star anise. Bring to a boil. Turn down heat and simmer for 5 minutes. Remove from heat and cool.

Renée Kelly's Harvest is at 12401 Johnson Drive, Shawnee Mission, KS; reneekellys.com.

Stuffed Sicilian Artichokes

CHEF/CO-OWNER JASPER MIRABILE, JR., JASPER'S RESTAURANT

"Do not be afraid to cook this delicious vegetable," says Chef Mirabile. "Just a little trimming and stuffing and you have an easy appetizer."

Prepare 4 artichokes by trimming the leaves down to where the inner leaves start to turn tender (using a serrated knife or kitchen shears), flat across the top. Remove stem, inner choke, and dry outer leaves. Boil artichokes lightly in salted water for 10 minutes. Drain water and cool.

In a mixing bowl, combine 2 cups breadcrumbs, 4 cloves minced garlic, 1/2 cup grated Romano cheese, 1/4 cup water, 1/4 cup finely chopped parsley and 1/2 cup extra-virgin olive oil. Preheat oven to 350 degrees.

Once artichokes have cooled, part petals and fill with breadcrumb mixture. Place artichokes in a deep baking dish, then add about 1 cup water (enough to fill to about 1/8th the height of dish). Drizzle more olive oil on top of artichokes. Cover with foil. Bake 30-45 minutes. Serve warm.

"You can skip the garlic, parsley, and cheese and just buy seasoned Italian bread crumbs, but I prefer fresh ingredients," says Mirabile.

Jasper's Restaurant is at 1201 West 103 Street, Kansas City, MO; jasperskc.com.

Tempura Asparagus

CHEF BRIAN AARON, TANNIN WINE BAR AND KITCHEN

Buy fresh local asparagus from the farmers market or grocery store in spring and try this light dish.

In a mixing bowl, combine 2 cups all-purpose flour, 2 cups cornstarch, 1 teaspoon each salt, pepper, and baking powder, and 1/2 teaspoon baking soda. Slowly add seltzer water (carbonated water) until just combined. Allow batter to rest in the refrigerator for 1 hour before use.

Trim off woody ends of 20 asparagus spears. Heat 2 cups canola oil in a deep sauté pan on high heat or approximately 350 degrees. Completely coat asparagus in batter and carefully place in hot oil for 1-2 minutes until crispy. Drain thoroughly to get rid of excess oil. Serve immediately.

Tannin Wine Bar and Kitchen is at 1526 Walnut Street, Kansas City, MO; tanninwinebar.com.

Wasabi Mashed Potatoes

CHEF BRIAN AARON, TANNIN WINE BAR AND KITCHEN

Chef Aaron says this dish is a great side for tuna, steak, tofu, chicken or grilled mushrooms.

Peel 4 large Idaho potatoes, cut in half and boil until tender. Meanwhile, simmer 2 cups heavy whipping cream and 4 tablespoons unsalted butter in a pan.

When the potatoes are done, drain and air dry for a few minutes. In a mixing bowl, whip potatoes (using an electric mixer with a paddle attachment), cream, and 3 tablespoons wasabi paste together until smooth. Season with salt and pepper. Serves 4.

Tip: Wasabi paste is available in the Asian food section of most grocery stores. Wasabi, a Japanese horseradish, adds a sharp heat akin to hot mustard.

Tannin Wine Bar and Kitchen is at 1526 Walnut Street, Kansas City, MO; tanninwinebar.com.

Zucchini Hummus

CHEF AMBER SHEA CRAWLEY

Chef Crawley's cookbook *Practically Raw* demonstrates how raw foods can be tasty and easy to prepare. Crawley says, "For this light hummus, the mild taste of the zucchini all but disappears behind the assertive flavor of sesame seed from the tahini."

Use a blender or food processor to blend the following ingredients until smooth: 3 cups peeled and chopped zucchini, 1/2 cup raw or roasted tahini, 2 tablespoons lemon juice, 1 small peeled garlic clove,

1/2 teaspoon agave nectar or sugar, 1/2 teaspoon sea salt, and 1/4 teaspoon ground cumin.

Taste for seasoning, adding more salt if desired. Transfer to a small bowl or container and refrigerate for at least one hour before serving.

From Practically Raw: Flexible Raw Recipes Anyone Can Make *by Amber Shea Crawley,* © 2012. *Used by permission, almostveganchef.com.*

Arctic Char With Mustard Beurre Blanc

CHEF/OWNER AARON CONFESSORI, WESTPORT CAFÉ AND BAR/THE BOOT

"Arctic char is closely related to both salmon and trout and has many characteristics of both," says Confessori. If it is not available at your supermarket, ask if you can order it, or just substitute salmon or trout.

To prepare beurre blanc, heat 1/4 cup white wine, 1/8 cup white wine vinegar, and 1 teaspoon finely chopped shallots in a saucepan until the liquid boils. Lower heat and continue simmering about 10 minutes until the liquid has reduced to about 2 tablespoons.

Cut 1/4 pound butter into 1/2 -inch cubes. Keep butter chilled until the liquid finishes reducing. Next, reduce heat to low, add cubes of butter, 1 or 2 at a time, and whisk rapidly with a wire whisk. Repeat as butter melts. Remove from heat while whisking in the last few cubes. The finished sauce should be thick and smooth. Fold in 1 tablespoon whole-grain mustard and season with salt to taste.

Prepare char by liberally seasoning both sides of a 7-ounce piece, skin removed, with salt and pepper. Cook 2 minutes per side over a grill or hot sauté pan. Ladle 2 ounces of sauce onto the plate and then lay the char directly in the sauce. Serve with sautéed green beans and spinach.

Westport Café and Bar is at 419 Westport Road, The Boot is at 415 Westport Road, both in Kansas City, MO; westportcafeandbar.com.

Balsamic Grilled Hanger Steak

CHEF JUSTIN HOFFMAN, BROADMOOR BISTRO

Hanger steak can dry out easily and turn tough if overcooked. Chef Hoffman applies a savory marinade to tenderize the meat.

To prepare the marinade, combine 2 cups balsamic vinegar with 1/2 cup Worcestershire sauce, 1 cup brown sugar, 1/2 cup Dr. Pepper soda, and 1 tablespoon soy sauce. Mix until sugar dissolves. Place 4-6 hanger steaks (up to 8 ounces each) in a container that can be sealed. Pour marinade over steaks, seal container, and turn to coat. Keep in refrigerator 3-4 hours.

Meanwhile place 1/2 cup balsamic vinegar in a saucepan. Bring to a boil and reduce liquid by   half. Set aside to cool and thicken. Remove steaks from refrigerator and bring to room temperature. Preheat grill.

Remove steaks from marinade and season with salt and pepper. Place on hot grill over high heat. For rare, grill about 3 minutes per side (1-3 minutes longer depending on desired doneness), brushing with thickened balsamic vinegar. Remove from grill and allow to rest for a few minutes before serving.

Broadmoor Bistro, a student-run culinary program at Broadmoor Technical Center in the Shawnee Mission School District, is at 6701 West 83rd Street, Overland Park, KS. The eatery is open during the school year. broadmoorbistro.org.

Black Bean Quinoa Burgers

JAMIE MILKS, EVERYDAY ORGANIC COOKERY

Milks serves these vegetarian burgers on buns or tortillas. She tops them with cheese, sliced tomatoes, avocado, lettuce, and salsa.

Place 2 cups cooked black beans, thoroughly rinsed and drained, in a food processor. Pulse until chunky. Transfer to large bowl, add these ingredients, and stir until combined: 2 additional cups whole cooked black beans, 1/2 cup cooked quinoa (see below), 2 large eggs, beaten; 4 chopped scallions, 3 tablespoons chopped basil, 2 minced cloves of garlic, 1 1/2 teaspoons cumin, 1 1/2 teaspoons oregano, 1-2 teaspoons crushed red pepper, 2 teaspoons sea salt, and 1/2 teaspoon ground black pepper.

Preheat dry skillet to medium high. Scoop 1/2 cup mixture at a time and form into 1-inch-thick patties. Cook for 5-7 minutes on first side. Carefully flip and cook on the other side for another 5 minutes.

To make quinoa (yields 3 cups cooked): Add 2 cups water to a medium-sized pot. Bring to a simmer. Thoroughly rinse 1 cup dried quinoa and add it to the simmering pot. Reduce heat to medium low, cover and cook for 12 minutes. Remove pot from heat, leaving quinoa covered for 5 more minutes. Remove lid and fluff with fork.

Everyday Organic Cookery; everydayorganiccookery.com

Boulevard Pot Roast

CHEF/CO-OWNER JASPER MIRABILE, JR., JASPER'S RESTAURANT

Chef Mirabile uses hometown brew from Boulevard Brewing Co. to cook this savory pot roast. This dish smells delicious, he says, and any Boulevard beer will work.

Slice 1 medium onion. In a large pot, sauté onion in 1 tablespoon of butter over medium-high heat. Dust a 2- to 3-pound boneless rump roast with salt and pepper to taste. Next, dust with 1 to 2 tablespoons flour, and brown the roast on each side.

Add 1 bottle of beer to pot and cook about 30 minutes for each pound of beef. Add beef broth as needed. Add 1 cup baby carrots and 3 or 4 Yukon Gold potatoes for the last 45 minutes of cooking. Season roast with more salt and pepper as needed.

Add more vegetables if you like, or prepare a gravy with the beer pan drippings. Serve over mashed potatoes or creamy polenta.

Jasper's Restaurant is at 1201 West 103rd Street, Kansas City, MO; jasperskc.com.

Brioche French Toast

CHEF/OWNER AARON CONFESSORI, WESTPORT CAFÉ AND BAR/THE BOOT

Chef Confessori uses brioche to update a classic with fluffy results. Brioche is a French bread with high egg and butter content, which gives it a rich and tender crumb.

Whisk together 6 eggs, 1 pint heavy cream, juice from half of an orange, 2 tablespoons vanilla and 1/8 cup sugar. Cut 1 loaf of brioche into 1-inch slices. Submerge brioche in egg mixture for 15 seconds.

Grease a large skillet with a pat of butter. Over medium heat, add soaked bread, and cook for 3 minutes on each side. Take care to avoid burning. Serve immediately with your favorite maple syrup and whipped cream. Garnish with orange slices.

Westport Café and Bar is at 419 Westport Road, The Boot is at 415 Westport Road, both in Kansas City, MO; westportcafeandbar.com.

Brown Sugar Bacon and Cheese Curd Stuffed Burger

CHEF JOHN MCCLURE, FORMER OWNER OF STARKER'S RESTAURANT

Chef McClure sweetens the deal with this bacon cheeseburger, using brown sugar plus cheese curds from Shatto Milk Co.

To make the brown-sugar bacon, dice a 1-pound slab of bacon into 1/4-inch cubes. Render over medium-low heat until bacon releases some of its fat. Increase heat to medium-high until bacon browns. Drain fat. Add one tablespoon each water and brown sugar for each 1/2-cup of bacon in the pan. Over high heat, bring to a boil and "candy" the bacon 3-4 minutes. Remove from heat, let cool.

Divide 8 ounces fresh ground beef into two equal portions. Shape into patties 4 inches in diameter. Place 2 tablespoons brown-sugar bacon and 3 tablespoons Shatto cheese curds (or, as an alternative, shredded cheese) in the middle of one patty. Leave 1/2-inch space at edges of patty. Place second patty on top of first and pinch edges together to form one large burger. Chill in refrigerator one hour. Season with salt and pepper; cook to desired doneness. (Extra brown-sugar bacon can be reserved for future use.)

Starker's Restaurant is at 201 West 47th Street, Kansas City, MO; starkersrestaurant.com.

Caponata

CHEF/OWNER SANDI CORDER-CLOOTZ, EDEN ALLEY CAFÉ

Chef Corder-Clootz recommends caponata for use "as a dip, a pasta sauce, stuffed into a wedge of brie, topping for pizza, bruschetta, grilled vegetables, or even over your favorite grilled fish."

Preheat oven to 375 degrees. Cut 2 zucchini, 1 bunch of celery, 2 peeled eggplants, 3 tomatoes, 1 red onion and 1 yellow onion into 1/4-inch squares. In a large bowl, toss vegetables with 1/4 cup olive oil, 1 tablespoon chopped garlic, 1 tablespoon kosher salt, and 2 tablespoons black pepper.

Spread vegetables on a sheet pan and bake in oven for 45 minutes. Check doneness by sticking a knife into eggplant. It should be tender.

Place in a large bowl after baking. Add 1 cup golden raisins and 1/4 cup chopped fresh basil. Optional: Add 1 cup of either capers or Kalamata olives. Stir well. Season with salt and pepper if needed.

Eden Alley Café is at 707 West 47th Street, lower level of Unity Temple; edenalley.com.

Cheese Spätzle

CHEF MATTHIAS SEYFRID, GRUNAUER

Spätzle, meaning little sparrow, is a fanciful way of referring to the egg noodle dish common to the cuisine of Austria and Germany. Look for spätzle in the pasta section of the grocery store.

For garnish, slice ½ a white onion into thin rings. Dredge onion in a mixture of ½ cup all-purpose flour, 3/4 teaspoon paprika and a dash of salt. Heat 1 cup vegetable oil in a deep small pan over medium-high heat. Fry onion rings until golden. Remove from oil and set aside.

Slice ¼ of white onion in julienne cut. Melt 1 ounce butter in large saucepan over medium heat and cook onions until caramelized. Add 2½ cups spätzle (dried spätzle cooked according to package directions) and sauté until slightly golden brown. Add 6 ounces grated Swiss cheese.

Next, add 2 ounces white wine and stir to de-glaze pan. Reduce liquid slightly. Add 2 ounces heavy cream and let spätzle simmer until it has a creamy consistency. Season with salt, pepper and a pinch of nutmeg to taste. Garnish with fried onion rings and finely cut chives before serving.

Grunauer is at 101 West 22nd Street, Kansas City, MO; grunauerkc.com.

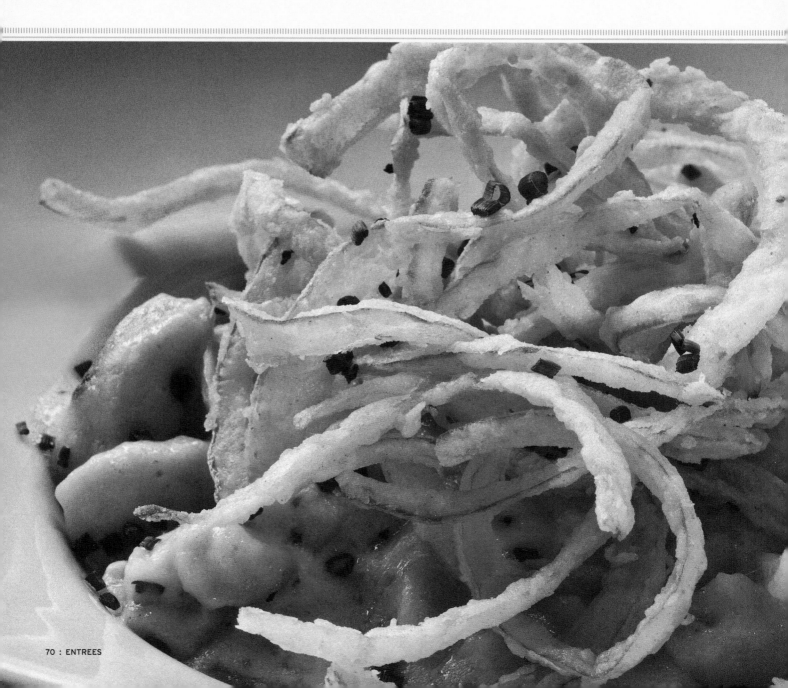

Citrus Halibut

CHEF/OWNER RENÉE KELLY, RENÉE KELLY'S HARVEST

Halibut, a lean fish with a mild flavor and firm white meat, can be broiled, grilled, smoked, and deep-fried. Chef Kelly marinates and sears halibut in a pan for a quick meal.

To prepare marinade, whisk together in a bowl the juice from 1 lemon, 1/2 cup olive oil, a dash of hot sauce, 1 teaspoon black pepper, 1 teaspoon lemon zest, 1 small minced shallot, 3 minced garlic cloves, and 1/4 cup chopped parsley, dill or basil. Marinate 2 (8-ounce) halibut fillets fillets for 10-30 minutes in the refrigerator. Heat sauté pan to medium high and add 2 tablespoons clarified butter. After butter is warm, remove halibut from marinade and sear on belly side first 1- to 2 minutes. Flip fillets and sear for 2 minutes. Turn down heat and cook to desired doneness. (Kelly garnished the plate with lemon zest, dill, shallots, and au jus from the pan.)

Renée Kelly's Harvest is at 12401 Johnson Drive, Shawnee Mission, KS; reneekellys.com.

Cowboy Mac and Cheese

CHEF ANDREW PARKER, MARTIN CITY BREWING COMPANY

This macaroni-and-cheese recipe has nothing to do with the pre-Revolutionary War tune "Yankee Doodle," riding on a pony, or sticking a feather in your cap (and calling it macaroni). Although it might inspire you to whistle the tune while making or eating the dish.

Cook 1/2 cup elbow macaroni according to package instructions, drain. Set aside 1 cup cooked macaroni (the half-cup dry macaroni should yield a bit more than a cup of cooked pasta).

Melt 1/2 tablespoon butter in a sauté skillet. Add 1/4 cup heavy cream and 1 teaspoon salt and bring to boil. Reduce for a minute on high heat. Add 2 tablespoons grated white cheddar and 1 tablespoon grated Parmesan cheese. Stir and melt together until the sauce has a smooth consistency.

Add 1 cup cooked macaroni. Stir for an additional 1-2 minutes. Place the pasta and sauce in an oven-safe dish. Spread 1 tablespoon grated Parmesan on top. Broil in oven for an additional 1-2 minutes, or until golden brown. Makes one serving.

The recipe's title comes from the enhancements Chef Parker makes to the basic recipe: He serves it at the restaurant with sliced jalapeno peppers, diced tomato, crumbled bacon, braised beef shoulder, and barbecue sauce on top.

Martin City Brewing Company is at 500 East 135th Street, Kansas City, MO; martincitybrewingcompany.com.

Crab and Spinach Quiche

SHERI PARR, THE BRICK

"Quiche is an easy brunch item that can be made ahead of time. They are quick and easy to make — and real men do eat quiche," declares Sheri Parr, owner of The Brick.

Prick a 9-inch deep-dish pie shell with a fork and pre-bake at 450 degrees for five minutes. Then set aside pie shell and reduce oven heat to 350 degrees. Drain a 4.4-ounce can of crabmeat or use an equivalent amount of imitation crab. Place evenly in bottom of pie shell 1 cup chopped spinach, crabmeat, 1/8 cup diced red onion and 1/4 cup chopped sweet red bell pepper. Cover with 1 cup shredded Swiss cheese.

Beat 4 eggs well in a small bowl. Stir in 1 1/2 cups half-and-half (or milk), 1/2 teaspoon salt and 1/4 teaspoon pepper. Pour egg mixture slowly into center of pie shell so mixture spreads evenly. Bake at 350 degrees for 35-45 minutes until golden brown or until a knife inserted near the center comes out clean. Let stand for 15 minutes, cut into slices and serve.

The Brick is at 1727 McGee, Kansas City, MO; thebrickkcmo.com.

Fish in Garlic Sauce

CHEF/OWNER BASILIO DE DIOS, LATIN BISTRO

Chef Dios aka Chef Tito prepares ajillo, or garlic sauce, for this dish ahead of time.* Guajillos, mild dried red peppers with a fruity taste, are available at most grocery stores in the produce or Hispanic food section.

Prepare ajillo by heating a large pan on low heat and adding 2 cups olive oil. Add 2 peeled heads of coarsely chopped garlic and cook for 2 minutes. Remove, cool, add 4 guajillos peppers and a pinch of salt and pepper, and store until ready to use.

To prepare the fish, warm 2 tablespoons olive oil in a sauté pan on medium-high heat. Season 1-2 cups flour with salt, pepper, and cayenne pepper to taste. Coat 3 fish fillets (such as tilapia) in seasoned flour. Place fillets in pan and cook until halfway done or nearly opaque.

Flip fish in the pan. Add ajillo to taste, along with 1 cup white wine. Finish cooking fish.

Plate the fish with ajillo on the top. Serve it with sides such as rice and vegetables.

*Johnson County K-State Research and Extension experts say flavored vinegars and oils should be refrigerated to avoid risk of botulism. They can also be stored safely in the freezer for several months.

Latin Bistro is at 6924 North Oak Trafficway, Gladstone, MO; latinbistrokc.com.

Italian Pot Roast with Gnocchi

CHEF TATE ROBERTS, EBT RESTAURANT

Chef Roberts prepares this dish to tender perfection using a slow cooking process on the stovetop.

In a large deep pot with a lid, heat 2 tablespoons olive oil and brown a 4-5-pound chuck roast on all sides. Add 1/2 cup diced white onion, 1/4 cup diced carrot, and 1/4 cup diced green bell pepper. Sauté until vegetables start to brown. Add 2 cups tomato sauce, 1 cup diced tomato, 1/4 cup tomato paste, 3 tablespoons dry oregano, 3 cups beef stock, 1 cup red wine, 3 tablespoons kosher salt, and a pinch of red pepper flakes. Bring to a boil.

Reduce heat to simmer, cover, and cook for 3 hours. Remove roast from liquid and set aside. Cook liquid until it starts to thicken a bit and yields about 2 cups of concentrated liquid. When beef is cool enough to touch, pull or chop meat into smaller pieces and add back to sauce.

Roberts suggests serving the roast with sautéed gnocchi pasta, risotto, steamed rice, potatoes, grits or polenta.

EBT Restaurant is at 1310 Carondelet Drive, #100, Kansas City, MO; ebtrestaurant.com.

Love Me Tender French Toast

SHERI PARR, THE BRICK

Inspired by Elvis' favorite sandwich of peanut butter, honey, and banana, Parr offers up this hunka, hunka (no burnin') love. Prepare this French toast in honor of Elvis' birthday (January 8) or when the craving arises.

Whisk together 2 eggs, 1 cup of milk, 1/4 teaspoon of cinnamon, and 1/2 teaspoon of vanilla extract. Dip 4 slices of lightly toasted bread in egg mix. Add a pat of butter into a large pan over medium-high heat. Cook bread on each side until golden brown. Spread thin layer of peanut butter on toast. Top with sliced bananas and drizzle honey on top.

"Use your favorite kind. The thicker the better," suggests Parr.

The Brick is at 1727 McGee, Kansas City, MO; thebrickkcmo.com.

Pan Baignant

CHEF/CO-OWNER MANO RAFAEL, LE FOU FROG

Pan baignant is a traditional tuna sandwich made with French flair by Chef Mano Rafael, who hails from the coastal city of Marseilles, France.

In a large mixing bowl, incorporate the following ingredients: tuna in oil from a 7-ounce can, 1/4 cup Nicoise olives, pitted; 1 ripe tomato chopped, 1/4 cup of roasted, peeled, and de-seeded bell pepper any color; 1 hard boiled egg diced, 1/4 cup red onion, 1/4 cup chopped green beans, 1 boiled and chopped new potato, 4-5 anchovy fillets, diced; 2 cloves of garlic, thinly sliced; juice of one lemon, 4 tablespoons red wine vinegar, 5 tablespoons extra virgin olive oil, and salt and pepper to taste.

Slice 1 baguette lengthwise, heat until warm in a toaster oven or oven. Cut bread into four equal lengths for sandwiches. Drizzle extra virgin olive oil on bread and add tuna mixture.

"Et voila! Fix yourself a Ricard and pretend you are resting after winning a game of petanque," kids Barbara Rafael, Mano's wife and Le Fou Frog general manager.

Le Fou Frog is at 400 East Fifth Street, Kansas City, MO; lefoufrog.com.

Pork Chops With Mustard

CHEF/CO-OWNER MANO RAFAEL, LE FOU FROG

"This pork chop recipe is a staple at Le Fou Frog's family food table," says Barbara Rafael, wife of Mano and co-owner and manager of the French bistro. By family, she refers to the staff meal prepared and eaten at the end of the night. A whole chicken, cut into parts, or chicken thighs can be substituted for pork.

Season 4 pork chops, bone in or out, with salt and pepper and cut into pieces. Brown in a skillet over medium-high heat about five minutes. When browned on both sides, take out of the skillet and set aside for later.

Sauté 1 cup fresh chopped mushrooms, 1 diced shallot and 1 cup sliced carrots in skillet used for browning pork chops. When vegetables have softened, add 1 cup dry white wine to deglaze pan. Reduce heat to medium and simmer until liquid is reduced to half. Add 1 heaping teaspoon Dijon mustard and stir in 1/2 cup heavy cream. When combined, add pork and cook on low for 3 minutes. Serve with rice, mashed potatoes, or pasta.

Le Fou Frog is at 400 East Fifth Street, Kansas City, MO; lefoufrog.com.

Pumpkin Pancakes

SHERI PARR, THE BRICK

Get into the Halloween spirit at any time of the year with these spooky (not really) pumpkin pancakes. Give dear mummy a break and let the kids have ghastly fun making this monstrously easy recipe for breakfast or dinner. Brought to you by culinary countess Sheri Parr, these flapjacks are sure to leave everyone howling for more.

Combine these dry ingredients in a bowl: 1 cup all-purpose flour, 1 tablespoon sugar, 2 teaspoons baking powder, 1/2 teaspoon salt, 1/2 teaspoon ground cinnamon, 1/8 teaspoon nutmeg, and 1/2 teaspoon ginger.

In another bowl, whisk together 2 egg yolks, 1 cup milk, 1/2 cup cooked or canned pumpkin, and 2 tablespoons vegetable oil. Stir into dry ingredients just until moistened. In a mixing bowl, beat 2 egg whites until soft peaks form; fold into batter.

Brush large nonstick skillet with oil; heat over medium heat. Cook pancakes until bubbles form on surface of pancakes and bottoms are brown, about 1 1/2 minutes per side. Repeat with remaining batter, brushing skillet with oil between batches.

Serve with fresh sliced pear and honey or warm maple syrup. Makes approximately 12 pancakes.

The Brick is at 1727 McGee, Kansas City, MO; thebrickkcmo.com.

Sage Spaetzle With Pork and Spinach

CHEF/CO-OWNER CARL THORNE-THOMSEN, STORY

Chef Carl Thorne-Thomsen frequently serves spaetzle, which translates from German as "little sparrow." This small dumpling can be short and thin or small and button-shaped, depending on the tool used to form the noodle.

To make spaetzle, combine 3/4 cup all-purpose flour and 1/8 teaspoon kosher salt in mixing bowl. Stir in 1 egg, 1 tablespoon plain yogurt, 1/4 cup milk and 4 fresh sage leaves, minced.

Bring lightly salted water to a boil in medium saucepan. Press thick batter through spaetzle maker (or through holes of a colander) into water. Retrieve spaetzle from water after a minute, toss with a little grapeseed or canola oil, and spread on a sheet pan to cool.

Heat a large sauté pan and coat lightly with grapeseed or canola oil. Add 6 ounces (about 3/4 cup) pork shoulder (cut in 1/4-inch dice) and spaetzle to pan at the same time and brown lightly. Add 1 teaspoon minced garlic and 2 tablespoons minced onion. Sauté 1 minute. Add 1/2 cup chicken stock, 1 teaspoon lemon juice, and 3 tablespoons butter. Cook until liquid reaches sauce consistency. Add 1/2 cup spinach leaves, reserving a few for garnish, and season with salt and pepper. Divide spaetzle between two plates. Garnish with reserved spinach leaves dressed lightly in olive oil and lemon juice.

Story is at 3931 West 69th Terrace, Prairie Village, KS; storykc.com.

Spaghetti Squash Casserole with Turkey Italian Sausage

SHERI PARR, THE BRICK

A casserole refers to a type of dish as well as the food served in it. A modern food staple in Midwest cooking, casserole derives its name and heritage from an Old World French term for saucepan. Parr offers a refreshing interpretation of this catch-all dish.

Cut a 4-pound spaghetti squash in half lengthwise, scoop out seeds, drizzle olive oil on the flesh, add a touch of salt and pepper, and place cut side down on a baking pan. Bake 45 minutes at 350 degrees until tender. Remove squash from oven and let cool slightly. Remove squash from pan and, using a fork, scrape out flesh into pan.

In a large bowl, combine squash with 2 cups ricotta cheese, 1 egg, 4 cups chopped fresh spinach, 2 minced garlic cloves, 1 teaspoon salt, 1/8 teaspoon pepper, and 1 pound cooked ground turkey Italian sausage. Transfer mixture to a 9x13-inch baking dish, top with 2 cups (canned) diced tomato and sprinkle 2 cups grated mozzarella on top. Bake 20-25 minutes at 350 degrees until casserole heats through and cheese melts.

The Brick is at 1727 McGee, Kansas City, MO; thebrickkcmo.com.

Squash Risotto

CHEF/CO-OWNER JASPER MIRABILE, JR., JASPER'S RESTAURANT

Squash, an English word derived from askutasquash in the Narragansett (Algonquian) language, means a green thing eaten raw. Chef Jasper Mirabile of Jasper's Restaurant in south Kansas City cooks winter squash, an abundant and inexpensive food full of vitamins, for this creamy risotto.

Peel, remove seeds from and dice 1 1/2 cups squash, preferably butternut. In a large 4-quart pot, sauté 1 cup sliced leeks and 1 1/2 cups squash in 2 tablespoons of butter for 4-5 minutes over medium heat. Add 2 cups arborio rice and toast for 2 minutes. Add 1 cup white wine and reduce liquid until absorbed. Add 5-6 cups chicken broth, 1 cup at a time, stirring each cup until absorbed before next cup is added. This will take 18-20 minutes.

Remove from heat. Add 1 tablespoon butter and 1/2 cup grated Romano cheese and blend. Garnish dish with 1 tablespoon fresh marjoram or to taste.

Jasper's Restaurant is at 1201 West 103rd Street, Kansas City, MO; jasperskc.com.

Spinach Mushroom Loaf

CHEF/CO-OWNER SANDI CORDER-CLOOTZ, EDEN ALLEY CAFÉ

Chef Corder-Clootz shares this vegan recipe from Eden Alley's cookbook *Stir-Well to Heaven* (edenalley.com/stirwell.html). The cookbook also contains her recipe for coulee, the tomato-basil marinara used atop this dish. Otherwise, substitute homemade or store-bought marinara sauce.

Preheat oven to 350 degrees. Clean and de-stem 1/2 pound fresh spinach and set aside in large mixing bowl. Dice 1 large yellow onion and sauté in pan until translucent with 1 1/2 tablespoons olive oil, 1 1/2 tablespoons minced garlic, 1 1/2 teaspoons each of oregano and thyme, 1 teaspoon each of kosher salt and black pepper, and

1/4 teaspoon chili flakes. Remove from heat and pour mix onto spinach immediately; it will slightly wilt the spinach .

Add 2 cups cooked, cold brown rice, 3 cups breadcrumbs, 1/2 pound shredded tofu and 1/2 pound sautéed sliced mushrooms . Mix very well with hands. Form into a loaf even in length, height and width, on a sheet pan sprayed with nonstick spray. Bake 50 minutes. Let cool for at least 20 minutes to set. Top with marinara sauce. Serves 6 to 8.

Eden Alley Café is at 707 West 47th Street, lower level of Unity Temple; edenalley.com.

Sweet Duck Breast

CHEF TATE AUSTIN ROBERTS, EBT RESTAURANT

Chef Roberts uses this recipe for chicken and duck breast. He suggests serving this with sides such as fresh pico de gallo, roasted red potatoes or a baby spinach salad.

For the marinade, combine in a large bowl 1 cup apple juice, 1/2 cup grape juice, 2 tablespoons molasses, 1 tablespoon fresh thyme, 2 ounces bourbon, and a pinch of cayenne. Use half of the marinade on 4 chicken or duck breasts, 6-7 ounces each with skin on, for at least 30 minutes and no longer than 2 hours. Reserve remaining marinade for later use.

Preheat oven to 375 degrees. In a heavy skillet, brown poultry skin side down over medium heat until very dark. Turn meat to skin side up and add reserved marinade. Place skillet in oven to roast. Roast duck for 7 minutes; chicken for 12-15 minutes. Remove poultry from roasting pan and set aside. Reduce liquid over medium-low heat in a saucepan and serve with meat.

EBT Restaurant is at 1310 Carondelet Drive, #100, Kansas City, MO; ebtrestaurant.com.

Baked Caramel Apples

CHEFS MEGAN AND COLBY GARRELTS, OWNERS OF BLUESTEM

Pastry Chef Megan Garrelts uses seasonal apples to prepare this dessert.

Coat a shallow roasting pan with unsalted butter and sugar. In a bowl, combine 1/4 cup apple cider, 1/8 cup brandy (substitute additional apple cider, if preferred), 1 teaspoon vanilla extract, 1 teaspoon ground cinnamon, a pinch of ground cloves, 4 tablespoons unsalted melted butter, 1/4 cup sugar and 1/2 cup brown sugar. Mix well.

After peeling and coring four Braeburn apples, cut each one into four large wedges and coat well in sugar mixture. Place sugared apples in roasting pan. Pour remaining sugar mixture in pan to cook into caramel sauce.

Using a tube of pre-made sugar cookie dough, dot the apples with the dough until about 3/4 of the apple surface is covered. Lightly brush cookie dough with 1/4 cup heavy cream and sprinkle with two tablespoons cinnamon sugar.

Bake at 350 degrees until dough is golden brown and apple sugar begins to bubble. Serve apples warm with a bowl of ice cream. Garrelts suggests butter pecan.

bluestem is at 900 Westport Road, Kansas City, MO; bluestemkc.com.

Barbeque Peaches

CHEF/CO-OWNER JASPER MIRABILE, JR., JASPER'S RESTAURANT

"Fire up the grill, because this peach recipe makes an excellent barbecue side dish or served as a bed for vanilla ice cream. Just imagine the aroma. This just spells summer, " says Chef Mirabile.

Prepare barbecue grill. Peel, core, and slice 4 fresh peaches in half. Sprinkle with juice from 1 lemon. In a sauté pan, add 3 ounces butter, 1 cup brown sugar, 2 tablespoons local honey, and 3 ounces Amaretto. Heat 2-3 minutes until sauce begins to boil. Take off stove and baste entire peach halves with sauce and place them cut side down on the hot grill over medium-low heat. Cook them for about 3 minutes, turn, and then cook 2 more minutes. Serves 4.

Mirabile offers another serving suggestion: "Fill the grilled peach halves with Wisconsin buttermilk blue cheese and let it melt." Sounds peachy.

Jasper's Restaurant is at 1201 West 103rd Street, Kansas City, MO; jasperskc.com.

Beignets

CHEF JOHN MCCLURE, FORMER OWNER OF STARKER'S RESTAURANT

Who doesn't like a doughnut? Beignet, a French word meaning fried dough, is a culinary way of saying, "Laissez les bon temps rouler." Let the good times roll with this recipe from chef John McClure, former owner of Starker's Restaurant on the Country Club Plaza.

Dissolve 1 tablespoon dry yeast in 4 tablespoons warm water, and let sit for five minutes. Sift 4 cups flour, 1 teaspoon salt and 1/4 cup sugar into a mixing bowl. Add yeast, 1 cup milk and 3 beaten eggs. Mix with dough hook for 5-7 minutes until dough forms. Place dough in an oiled bowl, cover with a towel or plastic wrap, and put in a warm place. Let rise for one hour.

Afterward, move to a floured surface, knead two times and roll dough out to 1/2 -inch thickness. Cut dough into 2-inch pieces of any shape. Fry in deep fryer at 350 degrees for 3-4 minutes or until golden brown. Dust with powdered sugar and enjoy.

Starker's Restaurant is at 201 West 47th Street, Kansas City, MO; starkersrestaurant.com.

Burnt Honey and Balsamic Roasted Pears and Mascarpone

CHEF/CO-OWNER JASPER MIRABILE, JR., JASPER'S RESTAURANT

Chef Mirabile uses ripe pears in season and balsamic vinegar to add zing to this dessert.

Preheat oven to 400 degrees. Peel 4 fresh pears, cut in half lengthwise and remove core. Place 4 tablespoons butter in a large bowl along with 2/3 cup honey and 3 tablespoons balsamic vinegar. Mix ingredients.

Place pears cut side down in roasting pan with 8-12 cloves. Put butter mixture (you'll need to reserve some of it) on top of each pear; roast for 20 minutes. Remove pears and place on dessert platter. Discard cloves. Whisk remaining sauce and drizzle on top of each pear. Serve with heaping spoonfuls of fresh mascarpone cheese and garnish with fresh mint.

Jasper's Restaurant is at 1201 West 103rd Street, Kansas City, MO; jasperskc.com.

Chocolate Panna Cotta

CHEF/OWNER CELINA TIO, JULIAN

Chef Celina Tio of Julian in Brookside offers this sweet treat.

In a saucepan, heat 1 cup heavy cream with 6 1/4 tablespoons sugar and 1 3/4 tablespoons dark cocoa. Place 2 cups cold cream in large bowl. Meanwhile, add 2 teaspoons powdered gelatin to 1/2 cup cold water. Dissolve gelatin in the warm chocolate cream. When cocoa, sugar, and gelatin are completely dissolved, add to the bowl of cold cream. Stir until blended. Pour mixture into 6 ramekins and let cool in refrigerator until set, at least four hours.

grocery stores, or find a recipe online) sweetened with a little maple syrup or sugar.

"The tangy flavor of crème fraîche is a great complement to the sweet richness of the chocolate panna cotta," she says. "If you'd like to add another dimension to the dish, we have always topped the panna cotta with a little sel gris (gray sea salt) or fleur de sel (sea salt)."

Julian is at 6227 Brookside Plaza, Kansas City, MO; juliankc.com.

Chocolate Pot au Crème

CHEF/OWNER BETH BARDEN, SUCCOTASH

Chef Barden prepares a divine pot au crème (pot of cream), a type of creamy, rich custard. Try this on Valentine's Day at home or anytime you want to impress a chocolate lover.

This recipe uses a double boiler, but a nonreactive metal bowl placed over a saucepan of simmering water will work. Place 5 ounces finely chopped dark chocolate in the double boiler or metal bowl and gently stir until just melted. (Keep water out of the chocolate.) Add 3 tablespoons sugar and 1 cup heavy cream. Whisk until smooth and remove from heat.

Lightly beat 3 egg yolks in a medium-sized bowl. Slowly add small amounts of the chocolate while whisking vigorously to temper mixture. Adding too much hot chocolate too fast will scramble the eggs. Place combined mixture on the double boiler on a gentle simmer. Whisk for 5 minutes or until thickened.

Remove from heat and whisk in 1 tablespoon of brandy or Grand Marnier and a pinch of salt. Pour into small coffee or dessert cups and chill until firm. Garnish with fresh berries and fresh whipped cream. Serves 4-6.

Succotash is at 2601 Holmes,
Kansas City, MO;
succotashkc.com.

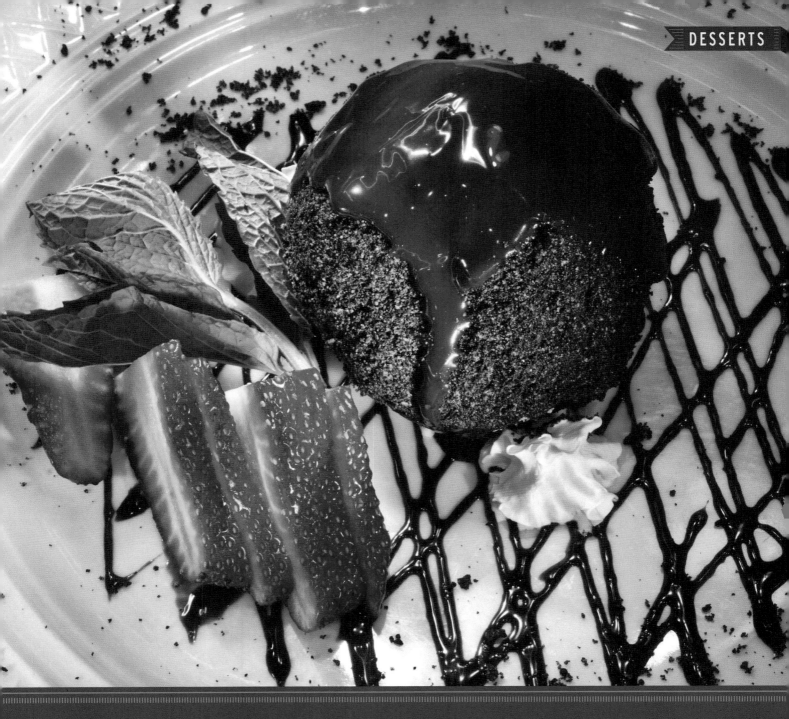

Chocolate Tartuffo

CHEF/CO-OWNER JASPER MIRABILE, JR., JASPER'S RESTAURANT

"This tartuffo is the perfect ice cream treat for summer," says Chef Mirabile. "You'll imagine you're in the Piazza Navona in Rome when you sit back and enjoy this dessert."

Scoop 4 ounces (1/2 cup) portions from 1 pint of vanilla bean gelato and form into balls using your hands. (Vanilla bean ice cream, or any flavor, can be substituted for gelato.) Make a hole in the middle and place 1 maraschino cherry inside, cover with gelato, and place on a baking sheet. Continue forming handmade balls with remaining gelato.

Roll gelato balls in 1 pound of grated chocolate or finely minced biscotti. Drizzle balls with chocolate syrup. Place in freezer for 15 minutes or until ready to serve. Serve with fresh whipped cream.

Recipe from Jasper's Kitchen Cookbook *by Jasper Mirabile. Used by permission. Jasper's Restaurant is at 1201 West 103 Street, Kansas City, MO; jasperskc.com.*

Chocolate Truffles

KEITH BUCHANAN, THE TEAHOUSE AND COFFEEPOT

Chocolate truffles are a treat for special occasions like an anniversary, birthday...or completing a load of laundry. Buchanan, who is half-British and half-Chinese, enjoys truffles with a spot of tea.

Grate or finely chop 8 ounces high-quality dark chocolate (70-85 percent cocoa is ideal) and place in a mixing bowl. Heat 1 cup heavy whipping cream to a simmer and pour over chocolate. Stir with a whisk until fully blended and smooth. Cover and refrigerate for 2-3 hours. Remove bowl from refrigerator. Use a tablespoon to scoop mixture and roll into 1-inch balls. Roll truffles in cocoa powder until coated. Store truffles in refrigerator. Makes about 1 pound.

The Teahouse and Coffeepot is at 4309 Jefferson Street, Kansas City, MO; teahousekc.com.

Five-Minute Blondies

CHEF AMBER SHEA CRAWLEY

This recipe for no-bake blondies produces a moist, nutty, and slightly crumbly dessert. "The vanilla, sugar, and salt marry seamlessly into a butterscotch-like flavor," says Crawley.

Combine 1 cup raw macadamia nuts or cashews, 1 cup raw walnuts or pecans and1/4 cup coconut palm sugar or brown sugar in a food processor. Pulse until mixture is coarsely ground. Add 2 teaspoons vanilla extract and 1/8 teaspoon sea salt. Pulse several

pulsing between additions until each date is well blended.

Transfer the sticky mixture to an 8-inch square pan (or similar-sized dish). Use fingers or a spatula to pack blondies into dish tightly. Refrigerate or freeze for at least one hour before cutting. Yields 16 servings.

From Practically Raw: Flexible Raw Recipes Anyone Can Make *by Amber Shea Crawley,* © *2012. Used by permission. almostveganchef.com.*

Grilled Banana and Blueberry Split

CHEF/CO-OWNER JASPER MIRABILE, JR., JASPER'S RESTAURANT

Chef Mirabile offers a modern twist on an old-fashioned recipe—and one that may transport you to the days of the drugstore soda fountain.

Prepare grill until hot. Rinse and dry 1 ripe unpeeled banana. Split in half lengthwise and drizzle cut sides with honey. Place banana cut sides down on grill. Cook 2-3 minutes until banana begins to caramelize. Remove from grill, peel, and place each half on opposite sides of a glass dish. Working quickly, place 3 scoops gelato or vanilla ice cream in a row between the banana halves. Drizzle scoops with 1 tablespoon each of caramel topping, heated hot fudge sauce and blueberry (or fruit-based) sauce.

Garnish banana split with 3 tablespoons whipped cream and top with fresh blueberries and 1 teaspoon chopped pecans. Serve immediately.

Jasper's Restaurant is at 1201 West 103rd Street, Kansas City, MO; jasperskc.com.

Honey Ice Cream

CHEFS MEGAN AND COLBY GARRELTS, OWNERS OF BLUESTEM

Pastry Chef Megan Garrelts uses only five ingredients to make this wholesome dessert. Try using local honey available at supermarket or select farmers markets. Recipe requires use of an ice cream machine.

In a large saucepan, combine 1 quart of heavy cream, 1/2 cup of whole milk, 1 cup of brown sugar, and 3/4 cup of honey. Warm over medium heat to infuse honey into the cream. Temper 12 egg yolks into the hot cream, adding small amounts slowly while stirring to avoid cooking yolks into lumps. Strain the mixture through a fine mesh sieve. Churn mixture in an ice cream machine and freeze until ready to serve.

bluestem is at 900 Westport Road, Kansas City, MO; bluestemkc.com.

Raspberry Chocolate Parfait

SHERI PARR, THE BRICK

This parfait sounds rich and decadent, but the use of part-skim ricotta and yogurt keeps the calories in check. But who's counting calories when dark chocolate is involved?

In a blender or food processor, puree 2 cups part-skim ricotta, 1/4 cup of honey, and 3/4 cup of plain yogurt. Fold in 1/4 cup coarsely chopped dark chocolate. Separate 2 cups of raspberries in equal portions and place into four serving glasses. Fill each glass with a quarter of the parfait mixture. Garnish parfaits with more chocolate and pecans. Serve immediately.

The Brick is at 1727 McGee, Kansas City, MO; thebrickkcmo.com.

Ricotta Fritters

CHEFS MEGAN AND COLBY GARRELTS, OWNERS OF BLUESTEM

Summer is a season for county fairs and crispy funnel cakes. These fritters, another type of deep-fried batter, are a winner in our book. Pastry Chef Megan Garrelts serves them with homemade honey ice cream.

In a mixer with a paddle, combine 1 egg white, 1 cup ricotta cheese, 1/2 cup semolina flour, 1/4 cup cake flour, 1/2 cup granulated sugar, a pinch of salt, 1 tablespoon baking powder and 1/2 vanilla bean, split and insides scraped into mixture. Mix until just combined.

Transfer the fritter batter into a quart container and chill until ready to prepare.

Using spoons, dollop spoonfuls of batter into a fryer or deep pan filled with hot oil. Fry until both sides are lightly golden. Dust heavily with powdered sugar and serve warm. Yields 2 cups of batter.

bluestem is at 900 Westport Road, Kansas City, MO; bluestemkc.com.

Skewered Strawberry and Marshmallow S'mores

KAREN ADLER AND JUDITH FERTIG, BBQ QUEENS

For this recipe, Adler and Fertig note that backyard garden strawberries are often smaller than store-bought, so you may need more.

Prepare a medium-hot indirect fire in the grill. Thread 3 medium-size strawberries and 2 large marshmallows alternately on each of 4 pre-soaked wooden skewers. Lightly brush 8 French baguette slices with olive oil. Place skewers directly over fire and grill for 4-5 minutes until marshmallows have browned.

At the same time, grill one side of bread slices, then flip them and move to the grill's indirect heat. Cut a 4-5-ounce dark chocolate bar in half. Break each half into smaller pieces. Place equal number of pieces on each slice of bread and sprinkle with a pinch of coarse salt. Remove slices from grill when chocolate is soft but still holds its shape. Serve skewers with grilled bread for a grown-up version of s'mores.

"Or even simpler," Fertig says, "grill strawberries on a rack until lightly charred and spoon atop frozen yogurt or ice cream."

Reprinted from The Gardener & The Grill *by permission of RUNNING PRESS, a member of Perseus Books Group. BBQ Queens; bbqqueens.com.*

Spiced Pumpkin Cheesecake

CHEF TERRY MILLE, COWTOWN CHEESECAKE COMPANY

Chef Mille prepares this decadent twist on traditional pumpkin pie, complete with a gingersnap crust.

Crust: Preheat oven to 350 degrees. Pulse 40 gingersnap cookies and 1/4 cup brown sugar in food processor. Transfer 2 cups crumbs to medium bowl. Add 5 tablespoons melted butter. Combine thoroughly with spoon and then with fingers until mixture is evenly moist and holds together when squeezing a handful. Press mixture evenly over bottom and partway up sides of 9-inch springform pan. Chill for 5 minutes, then bake for 10 minutes. Let cool.

Filling: Heat kettle of water. Beat 2 pounds cream cheese at room temperature with electric mixer until smooth. In separate bowl, whisk together 11/3 cups brown sugar, 1 teaspoon cinnamon, 1/2 teaspoon ginger, and 1/4 teaspoon each allspice, nutmeg, and salt. Add mixture to cream cheese. Beat until well blended. Add 4 large eggs and 2 large egg yolks one at a time, blending well before adding next egg or yolk.

Scrape bowl after each addition. Blend in 1 tablespoon vanilla and 1 (15 ounce) can solid-pack pumpkin (not pie filling), and stir in 1/3 cup heavy cream.

Scrape batter into cooled crust. Tap pan gently to release air bubbles. Set pan in larger baking dish. Add hot water from kettle to halfway up sides of pan. Bake at 350 degrees for 1 hour or until cake top looks deep golden and center sets. Cake will jiggle a little when tapped.

Turn off oven and leave door ajar for 1 hour. Remove cheesecake from oven and run thin-bladed knife between crust and pan sides to prevent cake from breaking as it cools on counter for 1 hour.

Cover and chill overnight. Serve with fresh whipped cream.

Cowtown Cheesecake Company; cowtowncheesecake.com.

Strawberry Balsamic Shortcake

SHERI PARR, THE BRICK

This light dessert uses a classic flavor combination of strawberries and balsamic vinegar to balance sweet fruit with tartness. Parr suggests baking Pillsbury pre-made biscuits for easy preparation. (Or use a made-from-scratch recipe.)

Wash 1 pound (approximately 4 cups) fresh strawberries. Remove caps and slice berries, then place in a bowl with 1/4 cup sugar and 1 tablespoon balsamic vinegar. Cover and refrigerate overnight.

Using an electric mixer, beat 1 cup heavy whipping cream, 1 tablespoon powdered sugar and 1 teaspoon vanilla extract in a medium bowl until peaks form.

To assemble, cut 4 buttermilk biscuits in half and place a large spoonful of strawberries on the bottom halves. Spoon whipped cream atop strawberries. Cover each with top half of biscuit. Drizzle juices from strawberries around shortcakes and serve. Makes four servings.

The Brick is at 1727 McGee, Kansas City, MO; thebrickkcmo.com.

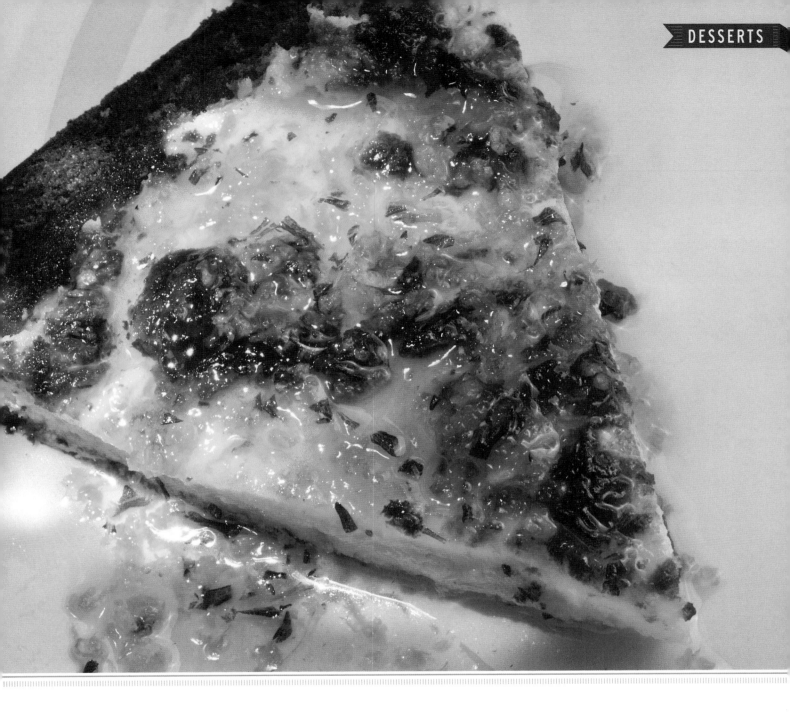

Turkish Yogurt Cake

JENNY VERGARA, TEST KITCHEN KANSAS CITY/VAGABOND

Inspired by her travels in Morocco, foodie and food entrepreneur Jenny Vergara shares this recipe. It is adapted from the cookbook *Arabesque: A Taste of Morocco, Turkey, and Lebanon* by Claudia Roden.

With a whisk, beat 4 large egg yolks with 1/2 cup superfine sugar to make a thick pale cream. Beat in 3 tablespoons all-purpose flour, then add 1 2/3 cups strained plain Greek-style yogurt, grated zest from 1 washed orange, and 1 tablespoon orange juice. Blend thoroughly.

Using an electric mixer with whisk, beat 4 egg whites until stiff and fold them into yogurt mixture. Pour batter into a 9-inch round, nonstick baking tin greased with butter. Bake at 350 degrees for 50 minutes. Cake will get golden brown on top, puff up like a souffle and then fall. Turn cake onto a serving plate. Serve warm or cold.

Vergara serves the cake with a homemade rosemary-orange syrup, but a simple sugar glaze will add sweetness if desired.

Test Kitchen Kansas City; testkitchenkc.com.

Vegan Bread Pudding

CHEF/CO-OWNER SANDI CORDER-CLOOTZ, EDEN ALLEY

Chef Corder-Clootz invented this recipe to use day-old bread. Ener-G® Foods brand egg replacer and vegan bread are available at Whole Foods.

In a large metal mixing bowl, add 4 tablespoons Ener-G® Foods brand egg replacer, 1/3 cup granulated sugar, 2 cups brown sugar, 1 teaspoon vanilla extract, and pinch of kosher salt. Whisk well until there are no clumps. Add 4 cups of soy, hemp, or rice milk. Whisk or use an immersion blender.

Add 1 pound of vegan bread sliced into 1/2-inch cubes. Mix with clean hands to coat all cubes in liquid. Melt 1/2 cup of coconut oil or soy butter on stove in a small pot or skillet. Let cool 10 minutes and pour over mixture. Add 2 teaspoons cinnamon and 1 16-oz package of vegan chocolate chips. Let mixture sit for 30 minutes.

Preheat oven to 350 degrees. Spray a 9x13 baking pan with nonstick spray and pour in mixture. Press with hands to level cubes. Spray one side of a piece of parchment paper and place coated side down on cubes. Cover

pan with aluminum foil and cinch edges. Place this pan onto a sheet pan. Bake 45 minutes at 350 degrees.

Carefully remove foil and parchment paper from hot dish. Place the dish in oven for 20 minutes and then remove and cool for 20 minutes. Choose a platter larger than the pudding. Place platter on top of pudding and carefully flip. Let sit for 10 minutes, then carefully lift pan from platter. Serve with ice cream or whipped cream.

Eden Alley Café is at 707 West 47th Street, lower level of Unity Temple; edenalley.com.

Chocolate Monkey

KEITH BUCHANAN, THE TEAHOUSE AND COFFEEPOT

Buchanan puts the fun in funky monkey with this drink for kids of all ages.

Blend 1/2 cup milk, 1/2 cup plain yogurt, 1 peeled banana, 3 tablespoons peanut butter, 3 ounces (almost 1/3 cup) chocolate syrup, 2 tablespoons sugar, and 2 cups ice. Blend together by hand until smooth.

The Teahouse and Coffeepot is at 4309 Jefferson Street, Kansas City, MO; teahousekc.com.

European Drinking Chocolate

KEITH BUCHANAN, THE TEAHOUSE AND COFFEEPOT

"This hot chocolate recipe is perfect for Valentine's Day," says Buchanan, a tea wallah or one who makes tea. He's also adept at crafting other potent beverages. "It's very rich and thick, with about twice as much chocolate as what I call 'American strength' hot chocolate."

Grate or finely chop 3 ounces high-quality dark chocolate (60-70 percent cocoa is ideal). Heat 1 cup of half and half (milk and cream) to barely a simmer in a small saucepan. Remove pan from heat, add chocolate, and stir with a whisk until blended and smooth. Serve immediately and top with whipped cream and/or marshmallows if desired.

The Teahouse and Coffeepot is at 4309 Jefferson Street, Kansas City, MO: teahousekc.com.

Farm Girl Cosmos

JUDITH FERTIG, BBQ QUEENS

Fertig uses a rosy rhubarb syrup in her cosmopolitans for a colorful cocktail with a down-to-earth twist.

To prepare syrup, place 4 cups chopped rhubarb (fresh or frozen and thawed) and 1 cup water in a saucepan over medium-high heat. Bring to a boil, then reduce heat to medium-low, cover pan and cook rhubarb about 10 minutes until tender and pulpy.

Strain pulp and reserve juice. Measure juice and add enough water to equal 2 cups. Return liquid to saucepan over medium-high heat and stir in 2 cups sugar. Boil until sugar dissolves, about 8 minutes. Remove from heat, stir in juice from 2 lemons and let cool. Strain again, then pour into clean glass jars or bottles. (Refrigerate, covered, for up to 1 month.)

For the cosmos, combine 1 cup rhubarb syrup, 3/4 cup vodka, 1/4 cup fresh lime juice, and 1 teaspoon orange extract in a pitcher. Add ice and stir well. Strain and pour into each glass or enjoy over ice. Makes 4 drinks.

"If you like, serve a trimmed stalk of rainbow chard as a swizzle stick," Fertig suggests.

Recipe from Heartland: The Cookbook *by Judith Fertig. Reprinted with permission of Andrews McMeel Publishing, LLC. Judith Fertig, BBQ Queens;* bbqqueens.com.

Hot Chocolate with Bourbon Meringue

CHEFS MEGAN AND COLBY GARRELTS, OWNERS OF BLUESTEM

Chef Garrelts' hot chocolate recipe, served with bourbon meringue, makes 4 cups and serves 8 good friends—the kind that will shovel your driveway during winter.

In a medium pot, boil 2 cups water and 1 1/2 cups heavy cream with 1/4 cup lightly packed brown sugar, 1 cinnamon stick, 2 star anise, 1 teaspoon ground allspice and 1/4 teaspoon ground cloves. Remove mixture from heat and stir in 10 tablespoons each chopped milk chocolate and bittersweet chocolate along with a pinch of salt. Steep hot chocolate for 10 minutes. Strain through fine-mesh sieve and discard spices. Keep warm until ready to serve.

Meringue: Whisk together 1 cup granulated sugar and 3 egg whites in a double boiler or heat-resistant bowl set over a pot of hot water. Simmer until sugar dissolves and mixture becomes frothy, about 3 minutes. Whip egg whites with handheld electric mixer on high speed until stiff peaks form, about 5 minutes. Add 2 tablespoons bourbon and whisk for 1 minute. Transfer meringue to piping bag and add dollop of bourbon meringue to each mug of hot chocolate. Serve immediately.

Recipe from bluestem: The Cookbook *by Colby and Megan Garrelts. Reprinted with permission. bluestem is at 900 Westport Road, Kansas City, MO; bluestemkc.com.*

Peachcello Liqueur

CHEF/CO-OWNER JASPER MIRABILE JR.; JASPER'S RESTAURANT

Chef Mirabile uses fresh, local summer fruit to prepare this versatile liqueur. He suggests serving it over sliced peaches, vanilla bean gelato, and whipped cream.

Peel, pit, and halve 4 peaches. Peel 1 lemon with a paring knife to remove the whole peel intact and then cut into 4 pieces. Discard the flesh or save for another use. Combine peaches with 3 cups vodka, lemon peel, 4 cloves, and 1 cup simple syrup in a covered Mason jar and store in refrigerator for 1-2 weeks, shaking occasionally. Strain out all solids. Place liquid back in Mason jar or decorative bottle and refrigerate. Serve chilled.

To make simple syrup, dissolve 2 parts sugar into 1 part boiling water and stir constantly. Once sugar is dissolved completely, remove pan from heat. Allow syrup to cool completely and thicken.

Jasper's Restaurant is at 1201 West 103rd Street, Kansas City, MO; jasperskc.com.

ANDREW PARKER   MARTIN CITY BREWING COMPANY

"My Dad raised cattle so I had a huge array of meat to cook," says Chef Andrew Parker, a Kansas City native.

He learned about different cuts of beef such as filet, prime rib, and shoulder tender. Parker loves to cook this cheap, delicious, and under-utilized alternative to tenderloin. Cooking beef at an early age influenced his choice of a profession.

"Most of my family worked in the medical field," he says. The kid with roots in the cattle business decided to be a black sheep. "I was drawn to restaurants so instead I chose cooking."

Parker began working in restaurants when he was 16. By 18, he was cooking professionally. He studied at culinary school and refined his skills at Woodside Health and Tennis Club, EBT Restaurant, and Hotel Phillips.

"Mentors Matt Quinn and Chef Tate Roberts taught me a lot," says Parker. "Cooking in a restaurant is a different beast, but I like getting good food in front of people."

Chef Parker has run the kitchen at Martin City Brewing Company since 2011. He produces upscale bar food such as the popular mac-and-cheese and risotto balls. Parker says, "It's classic comfort food that makes you feel good."
martincitybrewingcompany.com

AARON CONFESSORI   WESTPORT CAFÉ AND BAR

Aaron Confessori is the affable owner of Westport Cafe and Bar, The Boot Ristorante, and Westport Street Fare food truck. His Westport restaurants infuse a new energy into the entertainment district's culinary scene by offering bistro-style food with a French and Italian emphasis respectively. The food truck offers fresh ramen soup noodles and street tacos.

The establishments bring "an elevated sense of hospitality to a neighborhood setting," says Confessori.

Most of the time, Confessori oversees the dining room where he is most comfortable with the guests. His management experience landed him stints as General Manager at both Kona Grill in Kansas City and The Sea Grill in New York City. Before graduating from the classic culinary arts program at

the French Culinary Institute in New York, Confessori also worked as a line cook at Spice Market in New York City and as a sushi chef at Sakis in Scottsdale, Arizona.
westportcafeandbar.com

ALEX POPE   LOCAL PIG

Chef Alex Pope's current venture Local Pig is a locally-sourced butcher shop featuring whole animal, seam butchery, and artisan charcuterie.

Formerly, Pope worked as executive chef at R Bar and Restaurant (now defunct) in the Stockyard District and as sous chef at The American Restaurant. While at R Bar, he earned a 2011 *Food and Wine Magazine* nomination as the People's Best New Chef, Midwest Region. In 2011

he founded the pop-up restaurant Vagabond with Jenny Vergara.

Born in Peoria, Illinois and raised in Eau Claire, Wisconsin, Pope grew up in a family with long-standing culinary roots. The family founded the Antoinette Pope School of Cooking in Chicago. The school and its best-selling cookbook influenced Pope and primed his interest in food. He attended the University of Wisconsin-Madison and the Institute for

Culinary Education in New York City and earned a dual degree in Culinary Arts and Restaurant Management.
thelocalpig.com

AMBER SHEA CRAWLEY

Chef Amber Shea Crawley specializes in healthful and crowd-pleasing vegetarian, vegan, and raw food. She studied the art of gourmet living cuisine, also known as raw food, at the Matthew Kenney Academy, graduating as a certified raw and vegan chef in 2010. In 2011, she earned a nutrition educator certification at the Living Light Culinary Arts Institute.

Crawley was named Hot Raw Chef of 2011 by Living Light International. Her first

cookbook, *Practically Raw: Flexible Raw Recipes Anyone Can Make*, was published in 2012 by Vegan Heritage Press, and her second book is due out in early 2013.

Her simple recipes deliver an easygoing approach to living food, complete with cooked options. She says, "With my flexible approach, you can integrate health-promoting raw foods into your lifestyle at your own pace, even without special equipment or hard-to-find ingredients."

Recipes in Crawley's cookbook *Practically Raw* include almond butter sesame noodles, vegetable korma masala, primavera pesto pizza, cherry mash smoothies, and many more. In addition, she regularly posts free recipes, travelogues, product reviews, and other food-related fun on her website, Almost Vegan.
almostveganchef.com

BASILIO DE DIOS aka CHEF TITO LATIN BISTRO

Chef Tito, born Basilio de Dios, was raised in Merida, Yucatan. The influence of his mother and his Spanish grandfather, baker Don Vicente Garcia, fueled his culinary passion. He graduated from the Gastronomy IMSS in Merida, Yucatan.

Executive Chef Carlos Duarte, a 30-year veteran at Hotel Aluxes in Merida, mentored Tito early in his career. Tito gained experience cooking at Holiday Inn Hotels and Fiesta Americana

Cancun Hotels before working as executive chef at Restaurant D'Fernandos in Merida. He also worked at Restaurant del Lago, La Antigua Hacienda de Tlalpan, La Cava, and Le Moustache in Mexico City. He learned from Master Chef Jesus Alos Filigrana Maytredi at the Sheraton Hotels.

"Chef Maytredi was a wonderful inspiration and opened a window into the world of gastronomy," says Chef Tito. "He had the most influence over my career."

Tito's culinary style draws from the cuisine of Europe, Mexico and Latin and South America.

He owns Latin Bistro and Latin Bistro Express at two locations. He is a member of the American Culinary Federation and a professor at University of Missouri in Kansas City.
latinbistrokc.com

BETH BARDEN SUCCOTASH

Beth Barden become a flourishing small business owner and chef without any professional culinary schooling. She grew up with the folklore of a restaurant lifestyle spun from her grandparent's establishments in Detroit. Barden moved to Kansas City in the late 1990s.

During a career change, she began to cook at YJ's coffee shop. After steady encouragement from friends, she launched a catering company and later

opened Succotash in the City Market.

She moved her colorful restaurant and catering operation in 2009 to 26th and Holmes in Midtown. The expanded space allows room not only for her eclectic collection of local artwork and kitschy found objects given new life, but also for her larger-than-life generous personality. Of the vibrant and quirky decor, she says, "I'm surrounded by things I like."

Regular patrons from art school students to blue collar workers to mid-towners love her flavor-filled comfort food available for lunch and weekend brunch. The Cake and a Smile is a happy serving of a big buttermilk pancake with two sunny-side up eggs and a bacon smile. Her eight-layer rainbow cake is a signature example of her colorful style of delightful food that pleases the senses and the spirit.
succotashkc.com

BRIAN AARON TANNIN WINE BAR & KITCHEN

Chef Brian Aaron of Tannin Wine Bar & Kitchen has been cooking since he was five-years-old. He recalls when his mother asked what he wanted for breakfast one morning. "I told her that I wanted breakfast my way," says Aaron. "Then I pushed a chair over to the stove to cook."

At 15, Aaron began restaurant work when his older brother secured him a job at Sahara Cafe. The owner

showed Aaron some cooking fundamentals. Later, he attended Colorado State University where he studied restaurant and resort management and then attended culinary school at Johnson & Wales University in Denver. He also worked at Theo's in Fayetteville, Arkansas as a sous chef and executive chef and at Kansas City-based restaurants Starker's, Zin, and Parkway 600.

Now, Aaron uses fresh local products in a classic French meets contemporary approach that works in seasonal concert with the extensive wine selection at Tannin.
tanninwinebar.com

CARL THORNE-THOMSEN STORY

Carl Thorne-Thomsen's passion for cooking trumped his focus on creative writing while enrolled in a Masters of Fine Arts program at Wichita State University. "I lost direction with my writing," he says. "I kept thinking about food and became a student of the cooking process until it started to make sense to me."

Thorne-Thomsen and his wife Susan moved to Kansas City and started a family. He worked as a line cook at

40 Sardines and as chef de cuisine at Michael Smith Restaurant and Extra Virgin over nearly a decade.

After much planning, the couple's restaurant Story opened in 2010 in Prairie Village.

In part, Story refers to Thorne-Thomsen's being inspired by ingredients and the story he can coax out of them into a dish. He says, "The more time I spend looking for ingredients, the more I wind

up knowing about them, where they are grown, pastured, and fished."

The chef brings together ingredients like a story's characters and plot details. "I try to heighten the ingredients," he explains, bringing out their essential characteristics so a few items on a plate make an impact. "Each dish is simple and focused but not plain."
storykc.com

CELINA TIO JULIAN

Celina Tio's grandfather Julian put a chef's knife in the then-eight-year old Tio's hands and taught her how to use it right. Tio knew early on she wanted to lead a kitchen, thanks to her family's culinary influence and work ethic.

She worked in restaurants in her teens and later earned a degree in hotel and restaurant management from Drexel University. Tio started cooking at Philadelphia's Ritz-Carlton hotel. By age

23, she had been promoted to head the hotel's Grill Room.

Tio moved to Orlando in 1999 and helped open three specialty restaurants for Walt Disney World. Next, she arrived in Kansas City as executive chef for seven years at The American Restaurant. There she garnered recognition as 2005 Chef Of The Year by *Chef* magazine and the prestigious 2007 James Beard Foundation Award "Best Chef - Midwest."

In 2009, Tio opened an independently-owned restaurant named after her cooking influences: Julia Child and her grandfather Julian. The restaurant offers chef-driven twists on global comfort food such as paella, cassoulet, and pierogies that she calls "feel good food."

During 2011, Tio competed on Food Network's *The Next Iron Chef* and Bravo's *Top Chef Masters*.
juliankc.com

CHARLES D'ABLAING CHAZ ON THE PLAZA

Chef Charles d'Ablaing's cooking style incorporates regional bounty and sensibilities tied to his southern roots and ethnic influences. He hails from Atlanta, Georgia and spent a good amount of time in Savannah before moving to Kansas City.

d'Ablaing graduated from the accelerated program at the Atlanta School of Culinary Arts. Earlier in his career, he worked as executive chef

at Pearl Restaurant, The Webster House, and Hotel Phillips prior to his current role at Chaz on the Plaza in the Raphael Hotel.

The chef's emphasis on quality, locally sourced ingredients, proper seasoning, and precise cooking technique is reflected in a concise yet diverse variety of foods. Signature items include fried green tomatoes, shrimp and grits, and a hand-cut, wet-aged prime beef

tenderloin that advances Kansas City's beef reputation.

He was featured at the James Beard House in 2009 and has been prominent in local charitable events and competitions. His most recent event was the Chef's Classic Knockout Bout to benefit St. Paul Catholic School. He won on a split decision.
chazontheplaza.com

COLBY AND MEGAN GARRELTS BLUESTEM

Chefs Colby and Megan Garrelts met in the kitchen of Chicago's TRU, where they worked for chefs Rick Tramonto and Gale Gand. After working in kitchens in Las Vegas and Los Angeles, the married couple moved to Kansas City in 2003 and opened bluestem a year later.

Combining Megan's updates on classic American desserts with Colby's progressive take on regional food using the finest ingredients, often locally

sourced, the chefs have earned critical acclaim for their cuisine. Colby has garnered six James Beard Foundation Award nominations for "Best Chef - Midwest" and was named by *Food & Wine Magazine* as one of the Top 10 Best New Chefs in 2005.

The couple published *bluestem: The Cookbook*, co-authored with and photographed by Bonjwing Lee, in 2011. Cooking at home offers its own rewards.

Colby says, "Some of the best dishes are the ones cooked at home around our family table. When guests join us at home they become our family too."

Megan, who hails from Naperville, Illinois, and Colby, a Kansas City native, will open their second restaurant Rye in fall 2012 in Leawood's Mission Farms. The new restaurant will pay homage to Midwestern comfort food with a chef's "point of view."
bluestemkc.com

CRAIG JONES SAVORY ADDICTIONS GOURMET NUTS

"Thanksgiving 2005 was the first time that I had ever brined a turkey and then cooked it on the charcoal grill. That was the turning point," says Craig Jones. Since then he has been grilling and cooking over live fire between 300-340 days a year.

Jones has grilled everything from chicken Provençal to rack of lamb. "I love using smoke as a spice. Every wood gives a slightly different flavor,"

says Jones. "For each dish I make, my first thought is, 'How can/should I incorporate smoke into this dish?'"

When he started smoking nuts on a smoker, his hobby turned into a business. Jones and his wife Gay launched Savory Addictions Gourmet Nuts in October 2011 after their test batches prompted friends and coworkers to repeatedly ask for more. Made with all natural ingredients and

no preservatives, the blend of nuts – cashews, almonds, pecans, Brazil, and macadamias – are seasoned and smoked over wood in small batches. The resulting sweet, savory, and smoky flavor is hard to resist, as the addictive name suggests.

Savory Addictions Gourmet Nuts are available in over a dozen retail locations in the Greater Kansas City area.
savoryaddictions.com

DEBBIE GOLD — THE AMERICAN RESTAURANT

Chef Debbie Gold still seeks challenges to build on her two decades of experience. "If you are not continually learning, then you become stagnant," says Gold, winner in 1999 of the "Best Chef - Midwest" James Beard Foundation Award. "Cooking and food evolves. You have to stay aware of new techniques and philosophies."

Gold, a Chicago native, studied restaurant management at the University of Illinois, and then attended L'Ecole Hoteliere de Tain L'Hermitage in France's Rhone Valley. Afterward, she apprenticed for two years at Michelin-starred French restaurants before returning to Chicago to work at Charlie Trotter's to refine her skills.

She moved to Kansas City in the mid-Nineties to lead The American Restaurant kitchen as executive chef. *Esquire* named Gold a "Chef to Watch" in 1997, the same year she received the first of three subsequent James Beard Foundation award nominations.

In 2002, Gold opened 40 Sardines. The restaurant was nominated for "Best New Restaurant" from the James Beard Foundation. She eventually closed the operation and returned to The American.

In recent years, Chef Gold was a competitor on Bravo TV's *Top Chef Masters* in seasons two and four. **theamericankc.com**

DUANE DAUGHERTY — MR. DOGGITY FOODS

Veteran griller and barbeconnoisseur Duane Daugherty aka Mr. Doggity is a certified barbeque judge. His love of cooking goes back to childhood.

"When I was old enough to stand at the stove, my late grandmother put me to work in the kitchen. She instilled in me a passion for southern Missouri 'soul food'," says Daugherty. "I gravitated toward barbeque because it is KC's signature cuisine, but also because smoke is my favorite condiment. It is so complex and versatile."

He's traveled to all fifty states to sample, study, compare, and experience amazing barbeque. He says, "I created Mr. Doggity's BBQ Sauce as an homage to the best little places I visited around the country."

With over thirty ingredients used, the result is sweet and spicy with the tang of vinegar. He adds, "One local chef says he loved it because it has many layers of flavor, all in proper balance."

Look for Mr. Doggity's Southern Yankee rotisserie smoker, complete with pin stripes, 1950 Pontiac tail lights, whitewall tires, and moon hub cabs for a hot rod look, at catering events and BBQ competitions.

Daugherty hosts a weekly radio show called *Everyday KC* on BlogTalkRadio.com. **mrdoggity.com**

GRANT WAGNER — JJ'S RESTAURANT

Salina native Grant Wagner has come a long way since he began washing dishes at a small Lawrence restaurant. He was the sous chef at JJ's Restaurant for a year and a half. Wagner worked in several restaurants while studying anthropology, but then realized how much he loved the culinary lifestyle.

He found his calling at 4 Olives in Manhattan, Kansas. Wagner changed his career path and received an associate's degree from Le Cordon Bleu in Scottsdale, Arizona. He moved back to the Midwest to complete his degree with an internship at Kansas City's bluestem restaurant. Currently, he is the executive chef at JJ's Restaurant.

Wagner focuses on executing fundamentals of the restaurant's menu. "We have a solid menu that doesn't need adjustment," he says. "If it isn't broken, don't fix it."

In addition to serving featured staples such as steak, Wagner develops daily specials of fresh fish, pasta, and game. He says, "We have a lot of creative freedom to create specials."

Wagner continually works on his execution of classic dishes and learning his craft. He says, "I am trying to gain an encyclopedic knowledge of ingredients. I want to work with more local farmers." **jjs-restaurant.com**

JAMES TAYLOR — LA BODEGA

An old photo of James Taylor as a young boy in his grandmother Mary's kitchen now hangs in La Bodega on Southwest Boulevard. "I cooked with her as we religiously watched the *Galloping Gourmet*," says Taylor. "I always cooked with her and my mother, especially Saturday morning breakfast--my day!"

Taylor worked as a fourteen-year-old busboy at the Leawood Country Club. He was also a waiter and bartender while attending Kansas and Oklahoma Universities, where he studied architecture.

"That degree helped with design and structural problem-solving in every restaurant I have built," says Taylor.

He is the founder and former owner of 75th Street Brewery, River Market Brewery, Main Street Brewery (Cincinnati Group), and Re:Verse and The Red Room. He also founded La Bodega, a tapas restaurant with locations in Kansas City's Westside and in Leawood, Kansas. He is also an operational partner in Grinders.

Serving Kansas City diners a "Taste of the Good Life" matters to Taylor. "No one can travel to unique places all of the time," he says. "We want them to take a mini vacation, wind down, and be taken care of for a moment or weekend. Food and drink helps facilitate this." **labodegakc.com**

JAMIE MILKS — EVERYDAY ORGANIC COOKERY

"Cooking is something I have always done as long as I can remember," says Jamie Milks. "Growing up it was a way I bonded with people and expressed love. I have so many memories when I was young cooking with my dad, my step-dad, my grandma, and friends."

After Milks had children, she considered food quality with greater scrutiny. She bought produce at the local farmer's market for baby food and spoke with farmers there. "I learned about different growing practices," she says."I experimented with natural foods and fell in love with them."

Her family adjusted its diet after discovering the youngest son had a dairy and gluten intolerance and suffered chronic ear infections as a result. "In the process I found medical issues disappeared that I suffered from for years," says Milks. "I've had a lot of fun with learning to cook gluten-free."

Everyday Organic Cookery focuses on education and cooking classes. "I help people incorporate more whole foods into their diet and teach them how to cook," says Milks. "It is a skill not necessarily passed down between generations. I prepare simple, rustic food made with gluten-free, local, and organic ingredients. My goal is to redefine what 'healthy food' is to people."

everydayorganiccookery.com

JASPER MIRABILE — JASPER'S

Jasper Mirabile, Jr. grew up in the restaurant business. His grandmother helped his father launch Jasper's back in 1954, nearly six decades ago. Mirabile was named executive chef at the young age of 22. In his own style, he creates dishes from his own Sicilian background, along with a heavy influence from Tuscany and the Piemontese regions of Italy.

Mirabile says, "Living in the Midwest, I use numerous local farmers for fresh produce, beef, poultry, and dairy to create recipes with influence from my Sicilian background, carrying on the tradition my father started in 1954."

The nationally-acclaimed chef has made guest appearances at The James Beard House in New York and has cooked at restaurants in New York, Milan, Venice, and Paris. He has received extensive media coverage by major newspaper and magazines and once served as an ambassador for the Wisconsin Milk Marketing Board along with consulting and creating recipes for several major food companies across the USA.

Mirabile hosts the weekly radio program *Live! From Jasper's Kitchen* on KCMO 710. He has published two cookbooks, *The Jasper's Cookbook* and *Jasper's Kitchen Cookbook,* and is at work on a third, *On The Cannoli Trail.*

jasperskc.com

JENNY VERGARA — VAGABOND

Jenny Vergara, Foodie with a capital F, will be the first to tell you "there is no shame in that name."

She is the Table Hopping columnist for *Tastebud Magazine* where she offers restaurant recommendations and the author of The Making of a Foodie food blog. Vergara is the founder of Kansas City's first underground supper club called The Test Kitchen.

Her pop-up restaurant Vagabond was co-founded with Chef Alex Pope, owner of The Local Pig butcher shop.

"My love of food trucks is well documented," says Vergara. "I was an important catalyst for the creation of the Truck Stop, a permanent food truck lot in the Crossroads of KC located at 21st and Wyandotte. It is my goal to be the go-to girl for where to find great food and drink in Kansas City."

vagabondpopsup.com
testkitchenkc.com

JOHN McCLURE — STARKER'S RESTAURANT

Executive chef John McClure's dishes demonstrated key influences of his culinary style. Recipes such as Louisiana crawfish salad and peach salad with creole corn fritters reflected his experience cooking at Brigtsen's Restaurant in New Orleans. His farm-to-table cooking celebrated his upbringing on a Kansas cattle ranch and surrounding farmland. Signature dishes like the Tomahawk Chop, a bone-in ribeye, and brown sugar bacon and Shatto cheese curd burger were representative of his flair for presentation and use of local ingredients.

McClure, who died in 2011, had a tireless work ethic and generosity of spirit as a community volunteer.

Early in life, he cooked on the USS Independence while serving overseas in the Navy and trained at the Culinary Institute of America. In addition to Brigtsen's, he cooked at The American Restaurant and 40 Sardines before working as executive chef in February 2005 at Starker's Restaurant. In October 2006, he bought the establishment and put his stamp on the Plaza dining destination.

Starker's Restaurant, owned by the McClure family and operated by Chef Julio Juarez and general manager Dean Smith, continues to offer McClure's classic dishes and seasonal specialties.

starkersrestaurant.com

JOHN WESTERHAUS — WESTCHASE GRILL

John Westerhaus has nurtured a lifelong passion for cooking food and entertaining people. His interest in hospitality dates back to waiting tables in high school. Later in life, he operated a seven-location Subway franchise in Albuquerque. He sold the franchise in 2000.

To achieve his serious aspirations of becoming a chef and fine dining restaurant owner, Westerhaus packed for Paris to attend Le Cordon Bleu.

He studied cuisine and pastry and graduated with honors in both areas. "In France, I learned the beauty of simple recipes prepared with great ingredients," he says. "Buy the best ingredients you can, use the right techniques, and don't overdo the dish."

Chef Westerhaus draws on a range of influences to prepare the cuisine at WestChase Grille. He combines French culinary training with lessons, techniques, and tastes acquired while living and cooking in Colorado, New Mexico, and Texas. Whether it is a rustic dish using game meat, a touch of the Southwest, or classic French presentation, Westerhaus brings out the best in ingredients.

WestChase Grill also offers guests live music five nights a week. Westerhaus notes, "We feature some of the city's best entertainers from jazz to R&B." **westchasegrille.com**

JUDITH FERTIG — BBQ QUEENS (PICTURED WITH KAREN ADLER ON LEFT)

"Food tells a story that appeals to all the senses," says food writer and cookbook author Judith Fertig.

Fertig brings those stories to life through cookbooks such as *Heartland* (Andrews McMeel) and *Prairie Home Cooking* (Harvard Common Press). Fertig has authored thirteen cookbooks including *I Love Cinnamon Rolls* (Andrews McMeel) and with Karen Adler she has co-authored ten cookbooks on barbeque, grilling, and planking.

As the BBQ Queens, Fertig and Adler have cumulatively written over twenty cookbooks, including *The Gardener & The Grill*. It was selected as one of the top ten summer cookbooks for 2012 by *USA Today*.

Fertig's food writing has appeared in numerous publications such as *Cooking Light, Vegetarian Times, Better Homes & Gardens, Saveur,* and *The New York Times*. She also works in copy writing and recipe development for food corporations.

Her professional culinary training includes La Varenne Ecole de Cuisine in Paris and Le Cordon Bleu in London. She gives cooking classes across the country and has appeared nationally on radio and television. **alfrescofoodandlifestyle.blogspot.com thebbqqueens.com**

JUSTIN HOFFMAN — BROADMOOR BISTRO/TASTE

Chef Justin Hoffman is a culinary and restaurant management instructor at Broadmoor Bistro, a student-run kitchen and restaurant at Broadmoor Technical Center in the Shawnee Mission School District.

"As a former student of Shawnee Mission North and Broadmoor, I am proud to have the opportunity to come back and teach," says Hoffman. "I was part of the culinary and baking programs during my high school years. I spent the summer before college in Italy, studying their food culture and products."

Hoffman earned a degree from the Culinary Institute of America (CIA). He studied organic and sustainable agriculture in northern California. "In New York, I had the great pleasure of working with Chef Ken Ohlinger during my apprenticeship at the Lake Placid Lodge," he says. "I was fortunate to work and practice with the United States Culinary Olympic team at Westchester Country Club."

After his studies at the CIA, Hoffman catered weddings as the banquet chef at Devil's Thumb Ranch in Winter Park, Colorado. A year later, he returned to Kansas City to work as the general manager and executive chef of Taste restaurant in downtown Overland Park. **broadmoorbistro.com**

JUSTIN VOLDAN — 12 BALTIMORE, HOTEL PHILLIPS

Chef Justin Voldan chose his culinary career because he wanted a job that didn't seem like working. He began working at a family-run restaurant in Illinois where he learned from a culinary school-trained chef. Voldan gained knowledge and honed his skills at other restaurants, leading to a position at the Geneva Chophouse at the Grand Geneva Resort in Lake Geneva, Wisconsin.

As executive chef at 12 Baltimore since 2011, Voldan creates seasonal menus that take advantage of everything offered in Kansas and Missouri. He also leads the culinary team for banquets, catering, and special events.

"I enjoy seeing a customer's reaction to an expertly plated dish before they even taste it," he says. Further, he takes pride in presenting a dish that has been prepared and cooked to his high standards. What does he like most about being a chef? Voldan says, "There is nothing holding me back creatively with my menus and cuisine."

Voldan likes cooking seafood, especially scallops. He adds, "Another favorite is duck, especially since many people have never tasted duck prepared correctly. They are pleasantly surprised when they taste duck cooked perfectly."

12baltimore.com

KAREN ADLER BBQ QUEENS (PICTURED WITH JUDITH FERTIG ON RIGHT)

Food writer, author, and culinary instructor Karen Adler has a love affair with cookbooks. "I have to rein myself in when it comes to buying cookbooks," she says.

Adler is president and owner of Pig Out Publications, Inc., a wholesaler of cookbooks specializing in barbeque, grilling, and local Kansas City-authored books. Adler has taught culinary courses at FoodFest in Phoenix, A Southern Season in Raleigh-Durham,

Central Markets in Texas, Copia in Napa Valley, Marshall Fields Cooking School in Chicago, Smoke 'N Fire in Kansas City, and A Thyme for Everything in Lee's Summit.

She is the author of seventeen cookbooks with fourteen titles about barbeque. Her book, *Fish & Shellfish Grilled & Smoked* (Harvard Common Press), was co-authored with Judith Fertig and is considered the most comprehensive book written on this subject. The duo

have cumulatively written over twenty cookbooks, including *The Gardener & The Grill,* which has been featured in *Coastal Living* and *Country Living* magazines and on Martha Stewart Radio.

As the BBQ Queens, Adler and Fertig spread the word of slow-smoked barbeque and grilling through media appearances, special events, and cooking classes. **thebbqqueens.com pigoutpublications.com**

KEITH BUCHANAN THE TEAHOUSE AND COFFEEPOT

"I started baking as a kid," says Keith Buchanan, who was born in New Zealand, lived in Singapore, Malaysia, England, and Scotland, and at age 19 moved to the U.S. While attending boarding school in Galloway, Scotland, Buchanan helped to bake bread and cook in the kitchen.

He nurtured a lifelong interest in making and eating homemade foods. Buchanan says, "I pored over Marguerite Patten's *Everyday Cook*

Book in Colour and made cakes and scones."

Buchanan and his family opened The Teahouse and Coffeepot in 2010 next to their 42-year-old business Temple Slug. He prepares baked goods like rosemary-asiago scones and fresh dishes such as made-from-scratch hummus at the teahouse, where he shares his expertise on fine loose leaf teas.

"I'm half British and half Chinese so I practically have tea in my blood," he jokes. His favorite tea is first flush Darjeeling. "Good Darjeeling is transcendent. It transports me to another place."

His chocolate Guinness cake, adapted from a Nigella Lawson recipe, is a signature dessert. Buchanan says, "We made it originally for St. Patrick's Day. It's a crowd pleaser." **teahousekc.com**

LEON BAHLMANN CAFE TRIO

Executive Chef Leon Bahlmann draws on 25 years of experience and classic French and Italian training as he leads the kitchen at Cafe Trio. Earlier in his career, Bahlmann worked at Frondizi's, the Classic Cup, Harry's Bar & Tables in Westport, Cafe Maison, and Plaza III. His work experience built on a nine-month externship at the Ritz-Carlton during his two-year culinary program at the Culinary Institute of America in Hyde Park, New York.

"What really piqued my interest in this profession in my early 20s was the realization that the learning curve was pretty much endless and the subject matter endlessly fascinating," says Bahlmann. "A cook can work and study a lifetime and still not know half of what there is to know."

At the CIA, Bahlmann learned many facets of the industry. He met and worked with many types of people from different places. He says, "It has been a real blessing."

Bahlmann prepares new American cuisine with a nod to French and Italian traditions in the casual fine dining setting at Cafe Trio. Smoked lamb chops, pizza, monkfish, ceviche, and gnocchi represent a portion of the diverse menu.

He says, "We acquire the best ingredients we can, including local produce and products when available, and prepare them in ways that highlight their freshness and quality." **cafetriokc.com**

MANO RAFAEL LE FOU FROG

Mano Rafael, who grew up in Marseille, France, comes from a family of chefs. His mother Michelle, brother Jean-Roger, and Uncle Patrice Boelly worked in the culinary trade. At age 20, Rafael opened L'Auberge du Midi in New York's Greenwich Village with his brother. While there he met his future wife, Barbara.

Rafael also cooked at The Ritz Carlton, Petrossian, The Millennium, and Casanis in New York City. He received numerous

accolades while at Casanis. Ruth Reichl of *New York Magazine* described his chicken as "state of the art."

Mano and Barbara married, moved to Barbara's hometown of Kansas City, and opened Le Fou Frog (The Crazy Frenchman) in September 1996 near the City Market. The bistro's atmosphere is romantic, intimate, and dramatic. The owners and staff exhibit a passion for the arts, socializing, and

making the night come alive through food, drink, service, and sometimes a song.

Chef Rafael prepares authentic French fare and contemporary dishes that draw on the flavors of North Africa, the Mediterranean, and Asia. Le Fou Frog is known for its selection of game and seafood and the refined balance of flavors in Chef Rafael's dishes. **lefoufrog.com**

MATTHIAS SEYFRID GRÜNAUER

"I grew up in a very food-driven family in Germany's premier skiing destination Garmisch-Partenkirchen. Both of my grandmothers and my mother are excellent cooks," says Chef Matthias Seyfrid. "Family talk usually revolved around food. It was inevitable for me to become a chef."

Twenty years ago, Seyfrid, then 17, trained with two master chefs, a father and son, in a small family-owned and -operated restaurant in a town on the German/French border. Seyfrid says, "The father was truly a chef of the old guard. He taught me his philosophy which I go by to this day."

He worked as a chef de tournant, entremetier, and saucier at various hotels and restaurants in Germany. Seyfrid says, "I didn't know enough about chocolate, sweet baking, and the finer things in patisserie so I staged in one of Germany's best confisseries for a year."

After cooking in Switzerland, he worked in Vail and Denver, Colorado, where he met his future wife Erin. They moved to her hometown of Kansas City where Seyfrid landed at Grünauer as chef de cuisine.

He says, "My style of cooking is simple yet sophisticated, rustic yet elegant. I am a Francophile. There will always be a certain French factor to what I do. Foremost, it is to make people happy." **grunauerkc.com**

TERRY MILLE COWTOWN CHEESECAKE COMPANY

When Hurricane Katrina devastated the Gulf Coast region in August 2005, the Kansas City American Red Cross needed volunteers to help the population. Chef Terry Mille was emotionally riveted by television images of people being rescued from rooftops and losing their homes and livelihoods to the storm. Mille answered the organization's plea for help.

After volunteer training, Mille served as a mass feeding coordinator at Southern University. "I loved feeding hungry souls and getting to know people personally," says Chef Mille. "People told me about cooking with sweet potatoes, pecans they harvested, and handmade pralines they sold to New Orleans tourists to supplement their family's weekly bread money."

The experience changed Mille's life. Back in KC, he experimented with flavors and ingredients from the coastal region. Mille created a sweet potato cheesecake with gingerbread crust and praline topping for his family. Leftovers went to his wife's office where her co-workers placed orders for the cheesecake. Cowtown Cheesecake Company was born.

In 2011, Chef Mille prepared sweet potato cheesecake for First Lady Michelle Obama. "I focus on cheesecakes because I have found out that everyone loves them," says Mille, whose favorite cheesecake is strawberry. **cowtowncheesecake.com**

MICHAEL FOUST THE FARMHOUSE

Learning to cook with French techniques in the United States is a far cry from learning and applying those techniques in France. "I thought I was sound on technique," says Chef Michael Foust. "I worked with a saucier in France that had been making mother sauces for seventeen years. It was six months before I understood what he meant."

The process strengthened Foust's palate. He learned how to balance texture, flavor, and color when preparing a dish.

Foust built on a foundation of continuing education classes at Le Cordon Bleu by cooking in Portland, Aspen, Hawaii, New York, and overseas. Simply experiencing food offered lessons as well.

"I went to hole-in-the-wall tapas restaurants and bars in Barcelona," he says. "I found combinations that I wasn't familiar with at these mom-and-pop places."

Family ties brought Foust back to Kansas City. He opened The Farmhouse in 2009. His farm-to-table cuisine relies on strong relationships with farmers like Alan Garrison at Windhaven Farms. Foust says, "I couldn't do this without farmers like him."

Foust offers credit where it is due. Humbly, he says, "The Farmhouse is not a one-man show." **eatatthefarmhouse.com**

MICHAEL SMITH EXTRA VIRGIN/MICHAEL SMITH

Chef Michael Smith can peel ten pounds of shrimp in seven minutes - faster than anyone he knows. He has honed that speed and skill since the age of 12 when he began working in a seafood restaurant kitchen managed by his mother.

Smith graduated from the University of Southern Colorado. Then he answered a want ad for Chateau Pyrenees, a French restaurant in Denver where Smith studied under Chef Jean Pierre Lelievre.

"I liked the language of the kitchen and the hierarchy," says Smith. "I didn't know how to cook yet or run a restaurant, but I chose this opportunity."

In 1985, Smith traveled to southern France to learn about European cooking. Returning to the States, he worked as a sous chef at Charlie Trotter's in Chicago. He went to Nice, France in 1989 to be the Executive Chef at L'Albion. After stints in Chicago, he headed to Kansas City in the mid-Nineties. In 1999, he won the James Beard Foundation Award for "Best Chef - Midwest" while at The American Restaurant.

Smith's American cuisine reflects French and Mediterranean influences. His food preparation and presentation has evolved from the precision of French classicism to a more rustic style. **michaelsmithkc.com** **extravirginkc.com**

NATHAN FELDMILLER CAFÉ EUROPA

After graduating from college, Nathan Feldmiller moved Kansas City to New York to work at The Cub Room. He also baked at The Bouley Bakery and cooked at Restaurant Saul in Brooklyn, New York.

"I decided to move back to Kansas City where I opened a small deli called The Spot and then Circe on West 39th Street," says Chef Feldmiller. "When our lease was up, my partners and I decided take over Cafe Europa and expand the bakery business and start serving dinner."

Cafe Europa is a restaurant, bar, and bakery in the Crestwood neighborhood. Dishes range from wood-fired pizza to seafood and chicken entrees. Classic sandwiches like Feldmiller's take on muffaletta, reuben, and the Crestwood burger are a mainstay of the menu.

"I have always loved cooking and wanted to be in the restaurant business because I enjoy interacting with customers and being a part of a neighborhood," he says. "My culinary style is evolving, but always centers around simplicity and trying to present ingredients in ways that do not mask flavor, but rather accentuate the nature of an item." **cafeeuropakc.com**

PATRICK RYAN PORT FONDA

Chef Patrick Ryan opened the Port Fonda food truck in 2010 and served authentic Mexican street food. Two years later, Ryan and partner Jamie Davila opened Port Fonda as a popular full-fledged restaurant in Westport.

"With the restaurant, I wanted to create it in a new and different way as a collaboration between groups of people," says Ryan. He worked with local artisans such as Baldwin Denim and The Utilitarian Workshop to create a distinct look and feel for the business.

Ryan studied at Western Culinary Institute in Portland, Oregon before his internship at Frontera Grill in Chicago. He stayed in Chicago for five years, helped to open the W Hotel kitchen, and worked in other restaurants. After a stint at a restaurant in upstate New York, Ryan returned to his roots. "I hadn't lived in Kansas City full-time since 1993," he says. "There was a lot going on so I began checking out ideas for a new restaurant."

Kansas City is the beneficiary of Ryan's decision to establish Port Fonda as another invaluable addition to a diverse culinary scene. He says, "We have a concentration of celebrated chefs. We're lucky to have such great culinary talent here for a city of our size." **portfonda.com**

RENEE KELLY RENÉE KELLY'S HARVEST

After eight years of operating the event space Renée Kelly's in Caenan Castle, a restored castle in Shawnee Mission, Kansas, Chef Kelly converted the business in 2012 into a farm-to-table restaurant dubbed Renée Kelly's Harvest.

Chef Kelly prepares food using organic, locally grown, and farm-fresh foods where possible. She says, "The earth provides us with anything we need at any given point in time for optimum health, nutrition, and flavor."

Her dishes are inviting to the senses and as colorful and vibrant as her personality. She says, "Seeing the colors and breathing in the aromas of fresh ingredients are all the inspiration I need."

In addition to professional training in the culinary arts at Art Institute of Houston, Texas and an internship at Houston's River Oaks Country Club, Kelly worked stages with chefs Ming Tsi, Jean Joho, Michel Richard, Cat Cora, and Rick Tramonto. She was a guest chef on a Silverseas American Institute of Wine & Food cruise honoring Michel Escoffier's grandfather Auguste Escoffier, the father of modern cooking.

When not cooking or donating her time and talents as an active community volunteer, Kelly is writing three cookbooks. **chefreneekelly.com**

ROBERT BRASSARD BROADMOOR BISTRO

Robert Brassard began his culinary journey in a rural farming community in Connecticut. He learned how to can and preserve fruits and vegetables. He progressed from working in a local pizza shop to his first chef position as a nineteen-year-old working with Chef Dave Allen at Bald Hill Restaurant in Woodstock, Connecticut.

Brassard received culinary training at Johnson & Wales University and apprenticed in Vermont at the Fox Run Resort. Chef Brassard has been in the hospitality industry for over 30 years as a chef. He has been a certified executive chef for the past 20 years through the American Culinary Federation.

He works as a culinary educator at Broadmoor Bistro, a student-run kitchen and restaurant at Broadmoor Technical Center in the Shawnee Mission School District. Brassard has guided students in local and national culinary competitions over the past seven years, enabling them to earn over 1.6 million dollars in scholarship monies.

Brassard has been recognized as "Culinary Educator of the Year, 2008" by his educational peers at Foodservice Educators Network International. **broadmoorbistro.org**

SANDI CORDER-CLOOTZ EDEN ALLEY CAFÉ

Sandi Corder-Clootz grew up in a meat-and-potatoes family, but she chose to eat as a vegetarian at age 13. That lifestyle choice would one day become the focus of Eden Alley Café.

As a teenager, she worked as a hostess and in the back office at Jenny's Italian Restaurant. She learned about cheese from managing the deli case at a Price Chopper grocery store and later learned to cook at Californo's in Westport.

Corder-Clootz and her friend Monica Jones partnered in the launch of catering service Eloquent Jesters. When the minister of Unity Temple offered a chance to open a cafe in the lower level of the church, they seized the opportunity. Eden Alley Café opened in 1994 with an emphasis on vegetarian, vegan, and health-conscious food.

When Jones left the business, Chef Corder gained a new partner and general manager when she married Greg Clootz.

Today, Eden Alley Café offers traditional, organic, local, and synthetic-free ingredients suitable for raw, gluten-free, and other specific dietary needs.

"I was meant to cook and create with the fruits of this earth. My path was not planned, the route led me to this kitchen filled with love and peace. It led me to *Stir Well to Heaven*," writes Chef Corder-Clootz in the Eden Alley Café cookbook *Stir Well to Heaven*. **edenalley.com**

SHERI PARR THE BRICK

Sheri Parr, owner of The Brick for thirteen years, learned to cook from her father Ed. He didn't use recipes and was prone to experimenting with dishes. "We ate vegetables from his garden, fish, and game. He does not believe in eating processed foods," says Parr. "Everything on the table was from scratch. He takes great pride in the dishes he creates."

Parr's Italian grandmother Louise Graves owned Vic's Diner. Parr says, "She taught me a lot about owning a restaurant. She coached me everyday. I also learned from my employees. I have had the pleasure of working with really talented cooks."

Offering high quality food at The Brick is important to Parr. "I can't imagine not caring about what comes out of the kitchen. I want to put out food that I would serve to my own family."

At home, Parr cooks on her great grandmother's gas stove as time allows. "The stove is a great treasure to me. Generations of Thanksgiving turkeys were cooked in it. I love making red sauce on a dreary Sunday afternoon. I have also had the opportunity to cook for people on their sailboats in the Caribbean. I enjoyed this challenge, plus you're in the Caribbean sun!" **thebrickkcmo.com**

TATE AUSTIN ROBERTS EBT RESTAURANT

Chef Tate Roberts shares insight about the inspiration for his menus. "The inspiration comes from the seasons and the economy. I respect the customer's well being. Going out to eat shouldn't break your wallet," he says. "I'm a culinary historian interested in presenting classic food in a contemporary manner. Classics have to be prepared perfectly, even if they are deconstructed."

Roberts, executive chef at EBT since 2005, combines the rich heritage of food with rejuvenated modernism. "I am extremely emotional when it comes to food. Food and flavors come together for me very easily," he says. "My number one goal is to convey this passion to customers and my co-workers."

He earned a culinary degree from the Chef Apprentice Program at Johnson County Community College. Prior to EBT, Roberts worked at the Kansas City Marriott Hotel Downtown, Hotel Phillips, and Sheraton Overland Park Hotel. He took the Gold Fork home from the Taste of KC cooking competition two years in a row.

During a fundraising cooking demonstration for the Walk For ALS event in Kansas City, Chef Roberts said, "Food wants to work with you. Cooking doesn't have to be hard. It is a gift and a journey." **ebtrestaurant.com**

TED HABIGER ROOM 39

Ted Habiger began his restaurant career at the 75th Street Brewery in 1994 in Kansas City. He worked as a server, bartender, line cook and sous chef. In 1995, he progressed from a line cook to sous chef at Steve Cole's Cafe Allegro. In 1997, he was named chef de cuisine, and held the position for three years.

Habiger was reviewed by the *New York Times* travel section in December 1997, earning well-deserved accolades for Cafe Allegro. *The Kansas City Star* awarded him with three and a half stars the following year.

In May 2001, Habiger moved to New York City to work at Danny Meyer's renowned Union Square Cafe. He trained under James Beard Foundation Award winner Michael Romano and chef de cuisine Dan Silverman, and became sous chef in late 2001.

In 2003, Habiger moved back to Kansas City, working part-time at 40 Sardines while he launched Seasons Catering and Room 39 with Chef Andy Sloan. Focusing on seasonal, fresh, and locally grown ingredients, Room 39 has become a coffee and cafe destination in the heart of "restaurant row" in Midtown Kansas City. In 2007, Habiger and Sloan opened Room 39's second location in Leawood, Kansas. **rm39.com**

RECIPES BY CHEF AND COOK

INDEX